When Love Speaks

a collection to inspire
MAYA COMEROTA

When Love Speaks

mayacomerota.com

Published by Made to Change the World Publishing
Nashville, Tennessee

Cover and interior design by Chelsea Jewell

ISBN: 978-1-956837-04-9 Paperback
          978-1-956837-03-2 eBook

Printed in the USA, Canada and Europe

Dedication

This book is dedicated to the beautiful, brave, bold souls that listen to and act on that whisper for more. It is dedicated to the part of you that is seeking more love, more vibrancy, more passion, more joy, more aliveness, more connection, more purpose and more fulfillment. It is dedicated to the part of you that leans into fear and releases old, limiting stories to make room for the new, beautiful stories that you are creating at this very moment.

This book is dedicated to you and what is possible when love speaks to you and through you.

CONTENTS

FOREWORD

"I believe that the journey of life is about fulfillment of our heart's calling. It is about enjoying each moment and listening to the whisper of our heart to lead us on our journey."

— *Maya Comerota*

When Love Speaks is the written embodiment of just that . . . the whispers, the cries of the soul's messages of love—for self, for others, for the world. It is the culmination of dozens of journeys of self-exploration, self-expression and self-love.

Forty-four contributors—cantadoras and cantadors—storytellers and message-singers—have braved their trauma, shame and fear to discover their stories and share their messages of transformation. This book is a collection of those stories, of those messages that simply *must* be shared with the world.

Guiding each of these contributors through their individual journeys over the course of the past year was luminary, visionary entrepreneur and top transformational coach, Maya Comerota.

Maya is on a mission to unlock human potential—to help each person identify their X-factor—that gift that is uniquely theirs—and then empower them to live a life they love. Maya knows that when they become the person they were born to be and do what they were born to do, true living begins.

The contributors in this book now understand this too.

They successfully used the processes that Maya created to live their legacy now. As someone who's been on the journey herself, Maya knows the route. A brilliant leader, Maya takes the proverbial wheel and, with an outstretched hand, leads the charge, mindfully taking everyone with her. And while the road might at times be bumpy, Maya ensures everyone gets to their destination in class, in style and with a whole lot of fun!

Maya's heart, passion and unwavering commitment to never leaving a client behind—yes, 100 percent of her clients cross the finish line 100 percent of the time—result in a world-class community of clients who become family . . . who are each other's biggest cheerleaders. *When Love Speaks* is a beautiful representation of the love and loyalty that abounds among her clients. Once they enter Maya's world, they are friends, family, sisters and brothers for life!

The stories collected here reflect Maya's ability to open hearts and show the way to joy and deepest fulfillment. In her fun and supportive communities, she inspires and empowers her clients with the resources to reach their goals. But her determination and integrity ensure that everyone does the necessary work. She doesn't let anyone live in their own excuses. Yet, she leads her clients with warmth, helping them step into the person they were destined to be and create a life they love—a legendary life!

When Love Speaks is a testament to her results; the impact on and transformation of her clients is awe-inspiring. They know her heart; they know she cares. They know she creates a safe and powerful space that allows each person to rise in fulfilling their dreams.

And that they did! The contributors of *When Love Speaks* reveal the ultimate manifestation of the powerful love living inside each of us that—when sparked by a visionary leader—can ignite our potential, our purpose and our passions.

Ellie Shefi

#1 International Best-Selling and
Award-Winning Author, Entrepreneur, Speaker
Founder, You Are Not Your Scars™ and the
Made 2 Change the World™ Foundation

ACKNOWLEDGMENTS

The creation of this book wouldn't have been possible without the love and contribution of so many.

Thank you to the many beautiful contributors in this book—beautiful souls who are willing to share their lives, their stories and their hearts with me and with everyone who is blessed to read this book.

To my Living Legendary Mastermind Members—we have journeyed together this year on an adventure to create a legendary life full of love and prosperity, passion and joy, fulfillment and service. Thank you for joining me in *living your legacy* and not just leaving it. I thank you for trusting me to lead you and guide you on this beautiful journey of life. I am inspired every day by who you are and the ripple effect that you have on lives all around the globe by being you. My heart is so very grateful for you: Jenny Murray, Louise Taylor, Mollie McKiernan, Carmen Walsh, Carolina Migliaccio, Janet Annand, Jennifer Cavender, Kristin Zako, Lesley Rosas, Lisa LaFrance, Marina Haralanova, Patricia Lucero, Rasa DiSalvo, Jeannine Mullin, Shannon Reinhard-Chapoy and Terese Parkin.

To my Born For This Platinum Members and my Born For This Mentorship Members—you leaned into the vision that there is something you uniquely are born to do and trusted me to be your guide along the way. Thank you for opening your heart and spirit and sharing you with the world. You inspire me each day as you lean into your courage, authenticity and vulnerability. Thank you: Atiya Chaudhry-Green, Elayne Ireland, Gail Penny Dierks, Georgeta Geambasu, Gregory Mang, Jennifer Jubilado Sbalcio, Jennifer Poole, Jennifer Wallace Alvarez, Jenny Infante-Reyes, Judit Hora, Kathy Sweeney, Kelly Norton, Kerry Norton, Kim Bowers-Antolick, Laurette Smith, Linda Scherer, Lisa Treskow

Anderson, Marg Yungwirth, Martha Lubow, Mary Hinckley Tammaro, Michele Vayn, Michelle Delport, Michelle Golz, Michelle Lachner, Ramone Butler, Shelly Oberg, Sol Farias, Baudelia Reyes, Carrie Lynn Dann, Evelyn Galus, Julie Ann Janzen, Julie Moreau, Karen Scaffidi Barlow and Nancy Petersen.

To our Creator and Mother Nature for all the love and blessings of our lives and the ability to have love speak through us each and every day.

To my incredible husband, James, and my beautiful son, Hunter. It is your never ending support, love, grace and family cuddles that allow me to support so many others. You have shown me the true meaning of unconditional love. I love you both so very much.

To all of my family, especially my mom and dad. Thank you for your support, love and grace. I am me because of you, and I thank you for your love that you show in so many ways.

To my friends all over the globe: Thank you for your love and support always and for the adventure of life we get to have with one another.

To my beautiful friend and sister, Christine Burke. Thank you for your love, belief and support of me, our dream and the dreams and lives of so many. Doing life with you is magical.

To my team that makes this all possible. Thank you for holding me, my vision and my dream and the dreams of so many beautiful souls so that they may all come true. Thank you for sharing your incredible gifts with us all. You are a world-class team, and I am honored to partner with you: Christine Burke, Lesley Cameron, Jenny Infante-Reyes, Todd Cribari, Nathan Cribari and KT Ronshausen.

I am honored to have a few special contributors in this book that have touched my heart in many ways with their mission and their message: Sammy Taggett, Kate Butler, Sandra Estok, Lena Winslow and Colleen Low. Thank you for sharing your stories and your heart.

Thank you to my coaches and mentors who have breathed life into me and my dreams. To Mary Morrissey, John Boggs, Mat Boggs, Kirsten Welles and the Brave Thinking Institute for holding my dream and showing me that more is not only possible but it is inevitable when I come from my dream. To Bo Eason, Dawn Eason, Mary Kincaid, Jean-Louis Rodrigue and the entire Eason Team for showing me the importance of sharing our stories and how to show up powerfully every day as the person I was uniquely created to be. To Dean Graziosi and Tony Robbins for believing in me and showing me the power of sharing our message and our mission with the world so that I can support others to do the same.

And to Ellie Shefi and the Made to Change the World Publishing family, Stephanie Browning and Chelsea Jewell, for carefully and beautifully delivering these stories from each beautiful soul so they may be shared with the world. Thank you for making my vision and my dream a reality.

And I am especially grateful to each of you for reading this book, sharing our stories and listening when love speaks to you.

INTRODUCTION

What you hold in your hands right now are 44 love letters from 44 beautiful souls written for you and the world.

I believe that love speaks to us and through us in many different ways. For some, love is a feeling, a knowing, a tingle, a flutter. Love can be a whisper, a voice, a song, a touch, a kiss, a sunrise or a dream. Love appears to us in so many different ways—through connection with our Creator, with ourselves and with one another.

My intention in the creation of this book is that the stories and individuals inspire hope, connection, love and possibility. My hope is that this book supports us all to remember how connected we truly are. That your story is my story and my story is your story, and although we may not have the same life experience or believe the same things, there is love that connects and speaks through us all.

I believe that when you read the stories in this book, love will speak to you through the members of this beautiful community that came together to share their stories of trials and triumph, of hurt, loss, love, joy, miracles and dreams come true.

Last year, I asked the members of my community, "If you had just hours to live, what message would you want to share with the world? And what story have you lived that has provided you with that wisdom?" The answers to those questions are here in this book, *When Love Speaks*, which is a small part of the legacy that each person is leaving *and* living.

In this compilation, there are three sections dedicated to my mastermind members, my coaching members and a few special friends and contributors with a heart to serve the world in unique and beautiful ways.

Living Legendary is a group of beautiful women that came together on a mission to create a legendary life of joy, fulfillment, authenticity, vulnerability and prosperity. They seek to be the embodiment of their message and create a ripple effect of love through their being-ness each and every day. We have been on a journey for years, and I have the honor and privilege of being witness to the beautiful women that they are, the beautiful women they are becoming and the beautiful women that they have unbecome.

There is also a collection of stories from my Born For This Mentorship Members. This group is centered around the principle that you are here for a reason that only you can fulfill. Through the year, we have been navigating how to lean into that truth and be who we are each uniquely called to be. I am inspired by each of these members every single day and it is my absolute honor to share them with you.

Additionally, there is the Living Legacy collection of several beautiful souls with a mission and a message. They have each touched my heart, and I am honored to share their stories of how and when love speaks through them in this compilation.

In cultivating this book and curating the stories with each author, I fell in love. I fell in love with them, with their courage, their bravery, their authenticity and their vulnerability. And I fell more deeply in love with me as well.

As you make your way through the stories in the book, I invite you to open your heart and mind and allow love to speak to you through the pages so that you too can fall more deeply in love with you and this beautiful experience called life. No matter what your life experience is at this moment, I invite you to lean into *more*. More love, more passion, more aliveness, more compassion, more trust, more authenticity, more *you*.

I love you. I honor you. I celebrate you. I look forward to one day hearing your story of how and when love speaks to you.

Maya Comotota

"If I live through this
I will be the woman I was born to be.
I will live the life I was meant to live.
I will be her."

Be Her Now
Maya Comerota

When I was a little girl growing up in Elkins Park, Pennsylvania, I'd pretend to be Madonna and sing "Cherish" into my hairdryer while getting ready for school. In the afternoons, I was Eponine from *Les Miserables* belting out "On My Own" for anyone who would listen. And when my parents had friends and family over, no one could leave until they had congregated into the living room for one of my "performances."

I was going to be the first Broadway star that was also a doctor. I was going to live a legendary, exciting, fun life of musical adventures while also healing people, changing their lives and saving the world.

Twenty-five years later, after working hard to get good grades and working even longer and harder as an employee, I wasn't a doctor but I did have a new dream job: Head of Global Innovation for a fortune 100 biotech company, supervising a team of over 100 nurses who were supporting hundreds of thousands of patients with lifelong autoimmune illness.

I was making a difference *plus* I had a lake house, a boat, a shiny company car, a gorgeous husband and a beautiful son. Anyone peeking in the window of my perfectly decorated house would think, "Maya has it all."

What no one could see, though, was how much time I spent wondering, "Is this it?"

Why did it always seem like something was still missing?

I knew I was making an impact but I was still desperate for "more" even when I wasn't sure what "more" was.

Then on a beautiful sunny afternoon in August of 2015, I found out.

My 3-year-old son, Hunter, was playing downstairs with the nanny, Julia.

I longed to go downstairs and play with him. Just one more email I promised myself, then you can play. But that was over an hour ago.

Bing!

I get a text from Matthew, the VP of Strategy.

For months he's been sending me texts.

Come on Maya. Come to dinner with me.

Maya, we need to spend more time together.

Maya it's important I get to know you on a more personal level.

He knows the terms of my contract say that I can't quit or get fired without owing the company $250k so he keeps pushing, I keep saying "no" and he keeps getting more annoyed and upset.

Today's text reads:

Maya I'm with Tara. She's asking me what kind of job you're doing. Do you want me to tell her you're doing a good job? Or should I tell her you're not delivering?

Tara is VP of HR!

I can feel blood rushing through my body. I know I want him to stop but I don't know how to get him to stop. And I'm tired. Tired of him emailing. Tired of him texting me at all times of the day and night. I've barely been eating and sleeping because of this.

I keep saying, "I just want to do my job."

I've been at this company for 15 years. I've worked hard to get here, I have a team I love, I have a great pension, I'm making a difference and I want to retire here.

Why won't he listen?

Finally, my husband, James, and I go to see an attorney to find out what my options are. I don't want to cause trouble or sue the company. I just want Matthew to stop.

The attorney tells us, "Your case is open and shut. You've done nothing wrong but if and when you report this, your career is over."

I remember looking at James and thinking, "Maybe he'll stop."

That was three weeks ago.

I desperately wanted to be playing downstairs with Hunter, but instead I'm in my office afraid to move.

I have to get away, to escape, to get some perspective and think for a minute.

I grab the keys to my husband's truck and call out, "Hunter, mommy will be back in an hour."

"Mommy, mommy, take me with you," he says, with outstretched arms.

"No, little man. Mommy will be back soon. You stay here and play with Julia."

Twenty minutes later, I somehow passed my exit and I'm stopped at a red light wondering, "How did I get here?" I can't remember the last 20 minutes I've been on the road and I realize I am in the wrong lane.

As I turn the wheel to cross the lane and take the entry ramp back onto the freeway, a big, black SUV crashes into the side of my truck— right where Hunter would have been sitting!

The car starts to spin. Everything becomes slow motion.

The SUV crashes through the railing . . .
crashes through the green highway sign . . .
slides down the embankment . . .
comes to a stop . . .
seconds before hitting oncoming traffic.

I think, "Please God, don't let the driver die. Don't let there be a child in that car."

Then I see a vision.

It's Hunter, standing in front of James. They're both dressed in black, crying. My parents and brothers stand next to them. Everyone looks sad.

I hear a voice, or, more accurately, I feel a voice, in every cell of my body.

You did not do what you came here to do.

At the same time, I'm overwhelmed by the deepest sense of sadness I've ever felt.

Then another vision arises.

It's the day Hunter was born. I'm holding him in my arms, placing a gentle kiss on his head, promising to love him with all my heart.

I feel that love again. True unconditional love.

Then another scene.

This time it's my wedding. James and I are at the altar. He's looking at me with such love in his gaze before kissing me.

It's been so long since he looked at me and touched me like that.

A wave of regret washes over me. Regret that I haven't fully lived my life.

Yes, I've had fleeting moments of joy and love, but I knew I hadn't yet *really* lived.

That's when I make a promise, "If I live through this I will be the woman I was born to be. I will live the life I was meant to live. I will be her."

It was my first conversation with God and I was praying for another chance. The chance to do what I was put here to do.

When the police arrived, the other woman and I were embracing. The police looked at us and asked, "How did you get out of there?"

Both of our cars were totaled yet neither one of us had a scratch on us.

While I'm not sure how the other driver's life was impacted that day, I knew there was only *one reason* we had both survived.

That day changed everything. Not all at once. But little by little.

I knew I had to stop *doing* so much and *decide* to be the woman I was destined to be.

I didn't know exactly who or what that was yet, but I was determined to figure it out and I committed to myself that I would *Be. Her. Now.*

A couple months later, I was flying to Budapest to be part of a big global innovation meeting. I had routed my flight through London specifically so I wouldn't have to travel with Matthew, even though he hadn't been bothering me much since my accident.

Bing!

As we're landing, I get a text message from him.

I had them change your travel plans. You're staying two extra days with me so we can be together.

Adrenaline coursed through me.

"Be Her Now," I whispered.

I didn't want to be her. I wanted to run and hide.

"Be Her Now," I whispered again, then dialed my boss.

"Jack, there's something I need to tell you."

"Everything OK? Aren't you in Budapest?"

"Yes, but I'm getting on the first flight home," I said. "Matthew's been harassing me for the past six months. He keeps threatening to fire me if I don't do what he wants. I won't be at the meeting tomorrow and Jack, I think he may be doing this with others, too."

After a formal investigation, Matthew was fired. And, just like the lawyer predicted, my career as I knew it was over.

That January, after 15 years with the company, I handed in my resignation, my computer, and my phone and walked out of my office for the last time with my shoulders back and my head held high. I noticed the crisp, fresh air on my cheeks and the little gust of wind through my hair.

As I drove away, for the first time in years, I felt free. Free to be the me I was created to be.

I was no longer Maya, the Head of Global Innovation. I was just Maya. I wasn't even sure who that was anymore, but I knew it was up to me to discover who God put me on this earth to be.

"If there was no tomorrow, Maya, what would you do? Who would you want to be? What would you want to make sure the people you loved knew?"

The answer filled my chest and lungs and I wanted to scream from the rooftops.

"There is something you are uniquely here to do. Go, live your life, have fun, laugh, play, dance in the rain, sing! Be the person you are meant to be."

I didn't want anyone to feel the sadness and regret I felt in the car on the day of my accident, the regret of coming to the end of life and feeling like you hadn't really lived.

So my journey began. I listened to the voice that I heard and felt in the car and I let it lead the way.

It was peace, joy, compassion, love and faith speaking as a whisper in my body. As a swelling in my heart. Or a tingle in my nose. It was a feeling. A knowing.

When it gets hard, it will be okay.
You are never alone.
Your heart always knows.
Your dreams are your destiny.
Lean in to the longing.
You don't need to know the whole plan, just take the next step.
You are Born For This

When it rained, the whisper said, *Dance*. When a song I loved came on the radio, the whisper said, *Sing*. It told me what books to read, what lectures to go to, what courses to take.

At first it was hard to hear and sometimes even harder to follow. You want me to do what? You want me to go where?

But I learned to listen to its message. And the more I listened and the deeper I listened, the louder it became and the whisper drowned out any other noise.

I began to study and keep company with some of the greatest

transformational teachers in the world. I put pictures of them on my wall and had conversations with them in my head. I dreamed that one day I'd do what they do and impact people's lives at a grand scale. That simply by being who I am, and sharing what I came here to share, lives could be transformed.

It didn't come without challenges. My marriage was in turmoil, our bank account dwindled. We sold our lake house and my car. I even sold the suits I wore as a corporate executive, all the while whispering, through tears sometimes, "*Be Her Now. We're going to be okay.*"

Today, over a million people have been impacted by my programs and messages and I speak on some of the world's largest and most prestigious stages. But I never forget that every invitation that comes in to share my story and support others to change their lives is only because I dared to dream and first transform my own.

Hunter is now 10 years old and we have a morning ritual.

Every morning, Hunter calls, "Family cuddle!" and we all pile on the couch. Me. James. Hunter. And our wheaten terrier puppy who Hunter named Coco Comerota Stewart Bean McGee, or Coco for short.

Before he leaves for camp, I sing Hunter "Cherish" and he giggles.

"Mom, you're acting like you're 11 years old!" Then he busts out to take center stage, singing and dancing along with me.

"I love you, Mom." Then adds, with a big kiss, "You're the best mom in the world!"

James walks in and tries to wrap his arms around me while I continue to belt out notes and try to get him to dance with me.

Bing!

We're interrupted by a text from one of my students.

I was at a shop and it started to rain. Everyone took shelter but I ran into the parking lot and danced and twirled in the rain! It was so much fun! Thank you!

Even after all this, I still want more. But now it's a loving longing instead of a silent desperation. I realize that we will always want more, because we *are* more.

In fact, I have fallen in love with the desire for *more* as an expanded expression of self.

I still want more.

I want more of me.

And I want more of you.

Be. Her. Now.

PART ONE

Living Legendary

*"I embrace my sensitivity—it's my superpower
and my guiding light."*

Step Into Your Light
Louise Taylor

I owned the "crybaby" title in my family.

Growing up, my older sister, Joanne, loved to play *Let's make Louise cry*. I'd try *so* hard, but she'd always win.

My parents tried to toughen me up. "Don't be so sensitive!" they'd say. I didn't know how to do that, so I just stopped sharing my thoughts, feelings and dreams.

Instead, I focused on being great at *what* I was: first, an honour student, elite athlete and talented artist; then, a good wife, loving mom and successful marketing leader. I was an expert at helping *others* communicate.

But when you pulled back my curtain? I was an empty shell. I'd buried feelings and dreams so deep that I had no idea how to share them with my husband, family . . . or even myself.

Lord knows I wanted to, but when I tried, my head spun, my throat closed up and I literally couldn't speak. All I could do was cry.

At 41, my marriage crumbled. I became a single mom with two young girls.

Two years later, I developed pain in my jaw. It became so intense that I could barely open my mouth or even chew through bread. My dentist thought it was TMJ caused by years of grinding my teeth and clenching my jaw.

And if it was, there was *nothing* he could do for me.

Seriously?!? I thought, "I'll be living on baby food by the time I'm 50 and on pain killers for the rest of my frickin' life."

I paced anxiously in the exam room waiting for Dr. Blanas to give me the test results.

He started, "It's not TMJ."

Well, that was a relief!

Then he pointed to my CT scan on the lightbox and continued, "You have a tumor. It's growing on your bottom jaw inside the joint. The only way I can remove it is to take out the whole joint."

Wait . . . WHAT??? Sooo my jaw will be connected . . . yep, only on one side.

Shhhiiiittt . . . I had no choice. We did it.

I woke up from surgery with stitches all the way up my face, railroad track braces on my teeth and my jaw wired shut. I knew I had to relearn how to open my mouth, eat and talk. I had a long road ahead of me.

One day, I was in front of the bathroom mirror doing my jaw exercises. My face was still so bruised, swollen and sore. As I stared at my reflection, my eyes just welled up and tears started rolling down my puffy cheeks. I couldn't stop crying . . .

And then . . . OMG . . . I knew why this happened! It wasn't about healing bruises and relearning to eat. It was about me . . . finding my voice!

I didn't waste any time. A week later, I was sitting across from a therapist. She couldn't stop staring at my wired jaw; she was just so confused. "Uummm, *why* are you here?" I tried my best to explain through my clenched teeth: "I know there's more to me than what I am today. I need your help to find her."

That was 13 years ago.

Maya has shown me that there is no courage without vulnerability. Once I took that first step, my whole world began to shine.

Now, I share who I am with all my heart. I embrace my sensitivity— it's my superpower and my guiding light. And I'm living my dream: to help women entrepreneurs illuminate their heart-centered visions.

I believe that when we have the courage to step into our light, embrace our gifts and share our voice, *we have the power* to not only light up *our* world, but that of *everyone* we touch.

"My dream? It's on a faded vision board—a house, a beach and distant memories of my childhood holidays in the sun."

One Day or Day One
Jenny Murray

When I was little, my family would holiday at a tiny place by the beach. Mum, Dad, my three brothers and I would swim, build sand castles, run down the sandhills and, at night, play board games around a big table. We slept in and stayed up late. There were no chores and no homework. It was just *fun*.

And I would think, "*One day*, when I am grown up, I'm going to have my own beach house where my whole family will always have magical holidays together."

At 23, I married Alastair, who wanted to run his own cattle farm. Of course, I did everything I could to support him so that *one day* he'd be a successful cattleman, and then *one day* we could have holidays together with our whole family at our beach house.

As the business started to grow, so did our family: Callum and his fascination with dinosaurs; Caitlin, who would climb trees to see beyond the farm; and Brianna clip-clopping around in my high heels.

And *one day* this precious family of mine would all play and have fun in the sun.

One day, I sat in my office, reflecting.

Our business of 20+ years is really successful, and Alastair loves it.

The kids have all left home: Callum completing his second degree in Geology; Caitlin backpacking solo around the world; and Brianna starting her career in HR—all of them living lives they love.

What about me? My dream? It's on a faded vision board—a house, a beach and distant memories of my childhood holidays in the sun.

Why won't I start on something that is still so important to me?

And then Alastair came in and said, "We are buying another farm!"

My head dropped, tears welled up in my eyes.

Before I knew what I was doing, I shot up from my chair, stamped my foot and shouted, "Enough Alastair! Enough. What about what I would love—a house by the beach so I am not living where I work all the time? Somewhere so that when the kids come home, we can be together as a family?"

Alastair looked confused; he didn't understand. This was the first time in forever that he had heard me say anything about a beach house.

That year, Alastair got his new farm.

And me?

I got a beach house.

And it is so much more than what I had dreamed it could be—for me and our family. The beach house became a symbol for what is possible. Alastair started taking weekends off, and the kids all gathered to spend holidays together just like I had dreamed. And now, I am able to support others to believe that *more* is always possible.

I believe that if you are waiting for the *one day* to start creating the life you would love, well that day will never come.

"My soul whispered to me:
'You don't belong here anymore!'"

Here She Comes
Carolina Migliaccio

I grew up in a household where achievement mattered. I was "the artist." I wanted to have a career as a designer, but my dad envisioned me breaking the glass ceiling . . . in corporate.

It was Friday night; I just got home from a long business trip.
I put the key in the door like I had so many times before.
The TV was blasting.
My little dog cared to say hello.
The dishes were piled high in the sink, and I remember standing there . . . and my soul whispered to me: "You don't belong here anymore!"
But I pushed it aside, and I walked into the living room like nothing was wrong.

Over the next few years, I threw myself into my work and my career took off. Fifty was fast approaching, and I didn't want to be that woman at 50 with tons of regrets. So, *I decided* it was time to get divorced. Fifty came and went, and five arduous years later, I was finally free.

I was at the pinnacle of my career and was about to change jobs.
I remember walking out of Union Station on a gray day in Chicago.
I remember watching my bright blue Manolo Blahniks walk across the stone-gray pavement.
"I should be elated."
It was the final interview with the CEO, and I was going to arrive— the dream job that everyone would elbow me for.
Yet in that moment, I felt empty inside and I heard the whisper: "You don't belong here anymore!"
But I was standing outside the doors of this massive architectural creation.
Too late. I had to go in.
So I sucked it down, and I turned it on like I always did.

When I got home that night, I felt a heaviness inside me. I stared around my home witnessing everything that I had worked for.

This was my life's work.
My success.
But it didn't matter!

Because even though I had everything, I felt nothing.

How did I get here? And more importantly, why the hell had I stayed?

Yes, I wanted success, *but on my terms.*
And until I decided to take control and make the choice to be the pilot of my life, nothing was going to matter.
And so, in that moment, *I chose me!*
I decided to live my life.

I had no idea how to get there.
But what I did know was that I had everything I needed inside me.

It wasn't about starting over; it was about making the choice to create a new chapter.

I believe we all have the choice. We just need to decide!

And now, my life's work is to help others do the same.

We all have choices—the choice to stay in our pain or the choice to follow our heart. I believe that although our lives may seem like they're on autopilot, we all have a choice to live a life that truly inspires us. We need to follow our heart—it's our lighthouse, our beacon. Because when you make a choice to be in alignment with YOU— with what you truly desire and what sets your soul on fire—your life shifts from the shackles of "should" to freedom and abundance.

"I am changing the world with my little songs."

Sing Your Song
Carmen Walsh

When I was a kid, music felt like home, where I was safe and loved. It was a family thing. My mom was the church organist; my dad played saxophone. All five of us kids—me; my sister, Carol; and my three brothers, Nick, Eric and Ivan—learned to play at least one instrument. I played clarinet and saxophone in school, but it all started at the piano. I don't remember this, but my mom tells me that when I was really small, I sat on her lap while she taught lessons. When I got a little older, my favorite thing to do was play songs from her wedding collection. Singing beautiful melodies about love that lasts forever: that was my happy place.

But when I was around 10, that changed.

Eric, Ivan and I were eating breakfast at our kitchen table. Eric tipped backward and fell to the floor, his arms and legs jerking violently. "Please God, not another seizure!" His eyes rolled back in his head; all I could see were the whites. And I thought, "He could die; I could lose my best friend."

Well, not if I had anything to do with it! If I just took good enough care of him, he wouldn't leave me.

So I stopped playing and singing out loud! I needed to be quiet enough to hear when he fell, so I could run to protect him.

Eric died five years later.

By that time, I had forgotten how to relax. I didn't trust life without me controlling it. Music became just another thing to achieve in school until I stopped making it altogether. Instead of listening to and expressing myself, I listened for how I thought others wanted me to show up. And that's what I did—for the next 30 years.

One evening, I was in my kitchen washing dishes and half humming along with the radio, and I realized my life was pretty good. I thought, "If I can't relax and enjoy it now, when will I?"

So I started to sing out loud. It didn't matter how it sounded because I felt more alive than I had in years. The more I sang, the better I felt. I sang a Kenny Rogers song I loved as a little girl, called "She Believes in Me." It's about a musician and his girlfriend, who waits for him as he pursues his passion:

"I told her someday if she was my girl, I could change the world with my little songs."

It's funny, I used to identify only with the woman in that song—with the strength and sacrifice it takes to support those we love. But when friends told me they were touched or inspired by videos of me playing and singing, I realized I'm also the musician, and I *am* changing the world with my little songs.

I've come to believe the best way we can show up for each other is to listen to our own soul's calling, to allow ourselves to shine and to sing our own unique songs.

"I felt a new energy inside me; for the very first time, at age 37, I felt—a ZING!!"

Find Your Fit, Feel the Zing!

Mollie McKiernan

I am one of the youngest in a big family. This gave me instant lifelong friends, and it also gave me a lot of people telling me what to do most of the time. When I was about to go off to college, my siblings said to major in business because that was what women were doing. Of course, I followed suit. I convinced myself my dream was to become a fashion buyer. I think that was really my mom's idea.

I had arrived! I was in Manhattan on a buying trip fully coiffed in my fashion buyer attire. I completely looked the part. As I walked along the steamy back alleys, a dreadful, but familiar feeling rose. "Oh no, here it comes again!" Up my back, across my shoulders, around my neck and then, behind my eyes . . . the painful tears were about to spill over. You see, I was good at my job, but I felt lost and scared. I was a nervous wreck. I didn't feel like I fit in. I had to pretend, and I had gotten very good at pretending. I had mastered the art of pretending in my personal life. I was trying way too hard. I was exhausted!

I knew I had to get a handle on this anxiety, and I wanted to change, but I didn't know what that looked like. Something in my head kept saying, "If I just try harder, if I just work longer, everything will be okay." But no matter what I did, it didn't work.

One morning, I woke up and pulled the covers over my head. I just couldn't do this another day; I wanted to completely give up! I was living the wrong life, and I couldn't find a way out. (I was running and running, looking for the answer.)

I called my friend Mary, and through my gulping sobs said, "I can't do this anymore; I am so exhausted." After a calming peaceful silence, Mary started, "Mollie . . . " and then another long pause. And then, in her peaceful loving tone, she said, "just stop."

And I did. I just stopped.

I got a job in cosmetics to get by. The funny thing was, in cosmetics, the entire area is riddled with mirrors everywhere. I guess I couldn't hide from myself any longer. I started working with a therapist, which helped me take control of my life. I started to understand what I really thought, what I really felt and what I truly valued *for me*. I was getting to know myself . . . and things got better . . . slowly . . . day by day.

One day, the manager asked me if I would be interested in interviewing for a position in Human Resources. I looked up and said, "Yes I would!" I felt a new energy inside me; for the very first time, at age 37, I felt—a *ZING*!!

A new pep, a new energy! I knew exactly what to do. It felt like me. It was just easy. For the very first time, I not only heard myself, but I listened to myself, and I took action.

At age 47, I felt another *ZING*—a calling to adopt a baby from China.

And at age 57, I walked across the stage to receive my Master's Degree in Human Resources—*completely my decision that time*!

You see, I believe we all deserve to love what we do day-to-day. I believe we should get up each day and say, "I get to do this!"

Do you know the thing that gives you your ZING?!

"I felt like a kid again! I giggled to myself . . .
I couldn't believe I was doing this! It was pure joy!"

Get Your Hair Wet
Rasa DiSalvo

Eight years ago, I moved to southern California and got a small apartment steps from the beach—something I'd dreamt of for as long as I can remember. But because of my consulting job (that I'd long desired to exit), my hour-plus commute each way and never-ending client deadlines, I barely ever got to step onto that beach! My dream to live a peaceful beach life was so close, yet so far.

I could literally see the surfers through my window, but not *once* did I try to surf. As a busy mom and a professional, I convinced myself that I didn't have time to dive into a new, hard activity. Plus, the Pacific Ocean was way too cold anyway . . . or so I told myself. Secretly, I always looked with envy at those surfers riding the waves with so much passion, coming out of the ocean with the biggest smiles on their faces. A hidden part of me wanted to be out there as well.

One Sunday, I saw my girlfriend Angela coming out of the water with her longboard. "Wanna try?" she asked. A confident "yes" came out of my mouth, and I was immediately terrified of what I just committed to! She handed me her surfboard, but I felt as if she handed me some superpower. I grabbed that board and instead of tip-toeing slowly into the water and bracing myself for every step, like I normally did, I just started running! I frolicked into the water like I was in "Baywatch." I jumped on that board and paddled like I had seen other surfers do. I paddled and paddled . . .

Suddenly, a large wave rolled in, and the whitewash crashed all over me and my entire board. My whole body submerged under the water. But instead of feeling cold or tightening up, I felt so alive, so free and so one with the ocean. I got tumbled quite a few more times. I was barely able to stay on my board, but I embraced this magical new experience with every fiber of my being. I finally managed to pass the wave break and sat up on my board—in the middle of the ocean! I felt like a kid again! I giggled to myself . . . I couldn't believe I was doing this! It was *pure joy* to be out there! I wondered why I hadn't tried surfing years before. The answer could not have been any clearer . . .

It was my damn hair—I was never willing to get my hair wet. All those years, I would get into the ocean barely shoulder-deep and pat myself on the back for getting in at all—that had been good enough! I knew there was more to the experience, but I would stop myself from fully immersing because going under water felt just a little bit uncomfortable and a little bit scary.

And then I realized that I did the exact same thing in other areas of my life. My career was good enough, so I stopped myself from pursuing what my heart truly desired because making a change felt just a little bit uncomfortable and a little bit scary.

So in that moment . . . in the middle of the ocean . . . I decided to no longer tip-toe around life.

After that, I dove full-in and made that career change I'd so desperately wanted for years!

I believe life is meant to be *fully* lived . . . we just have to be willing to *get our hair wet*.

"I finally recognize what I couldn't see before—
the truth that we are all beautiful."

Unlocking *Your* Unique Beauty
Terese Parkin

I was blessed to grow up in a large family of eight children. Every night, we would get down on our knees and pray, "God bless Mommy, Daddy, Roseanne, Greg, Susie, Mike, Gerry, Terese, Frances and Bernie." I so loved our family, and I knew that I wanted to have my very own family like it one day.

I really thought the world would give me that same unconditional love.

I am 7 years old.

At school, Jimmy and Mike start a chant: "Terese looks like Buckwheat!" Do you remember Buckwheat? He was a character in the "Little Rascals" show. He had big eyes, big ears and big teeth, and his features just didn't seem to fit in his small face. Like me!

I just want to fit in.

In my teens, I struggled with social pressure to look like models in magazines and like my younger sister, Frances, who was naturally skinny.

I am 17 years old.

I stare in disgust at the image of my body in my bedroom mirror. What my eyes see is an overweight, frumpy and unattractive girl. My mom slips into the room and says, "Terese, what is going on?"

Her eyes see something very different. She's so worried that the next thing I know, I'm at the doctor's office. Dr. Lake sits me down, looks me in the eyes and says, "Terese, you are not strong. You barely weigh *100* pounds! You are too small and weak, and if you continue like this, you may not ever be able to have a child."

What!? Wait a minute—no way!! Me not able to have kids?! But having kids is all I've ever wanted!

These words jolt me to the core, and something clicks inside my head. I decide right then to begin eating again and make my health a priority.

I am 19 years old.

I meet the love of my life, Charlie. We marry and have our first child, Greg. This is the *best* day! Thankfully, we are able to have two more beautiful children, Lauren and Andrew.

We are happy in our marriage and raising our three kids. I have so much to be grateful for, and yet, I feel a burning desire inside of me—a *knowing* that there is a purpose that I am not fulfilling.

I am 59 years old.

I am attending an event where we are asked, "What is your greatest obstacle stopping you from living the life you are yearning for?" We share our reflections with the woman to our right. I turn to see a beautiful woman, Denise, who has warm brown eyes and beautiful blonde hair, and I instantly can tell she has a big heart. I say tearfully, "I don't feel confident, I don't feel beautiful and I just want people to like me." Denise, gripping my hands, says to me with tears running down *her* face, "*You* don't feel confident? You don't feel beautiful? That is me—and exactly how I feel! Just like you do!"

Denise was beautiful and couldn't see it. I realize at that moment that if she and I both feel this way, all the women at the event most likely feel the same way! *I finally recognize what I couldn't see before*—the truth that we are all beautiful.

I am 63 years old.

I now see that I had beauty in me when I was called names at 7 and when I had anorexia and couldn't see my true image at 17. And I know that I have abundant beauty now at age 63!

I believe that we are all blessed with our own unique and timeless beauty no matter our weight, circumstance, gender or age. It is when we recognize that we are born beautiful and when we share in joy with others that we live an ageless, beautiful life!

*"By writing and telling my stories,
I connect with myself, and I fall in love with me."*

Connecting the Dots to Love

Lisa LaFrance

Steve Jobs said, "You can't connect the dots looking forward; you can only connect them looking backwards. So, you have to trust that the dots will somehow connect in your future. You have to trust in something."

It's early 2020, and I am sitting on my porch watching the birds. They look so free and happy. Being able to fly would be so wonderful. I catch a glimpse of myself in the window. Where did the strong, smart, accomplished woman—the go-getter—go? The house behind me is so quiet. My beautiful son, Jordan, has left the nest to pursue his passion.

Now what?

My life looks great from the outside, but how much longer can I pretend? I am so desperate for more.

The phone rings. I have such a tingle in my belly as I answer the call.

Maya's name had been calling my name for a long while, and I sign up on the spot after talking to her. I hang up the phone, and I cry tears of relief. I don't really know what I signed up for! All I know is that I have a feeling of hope again. A tiny spark of excitement that all could be well.

And so it begins.

During one of our Zoom calls, Maya asks, "What is the message you want to tell the world, Lisa?"

"How do you know?" I reply. I don't yet know what my message is; I just know it has something to do with love.

"What do you love? It is time to pause and stop running," she says.

I pause and take a breath.

I get on our mastermind calls, and, week after week, I listen to all these beautiful women tell their stories. And I fall in love at first with their stories and then with them. I cannot wait to jump on our calls each week. I want some of what I see in them too.

As the due date for my story nears, I struggle to put even one word on a page. So, I go to the beach, my happy place, and, after rolling down the sand and laughing out loud, I am finally able to write.

The other women work on one story, and I write and I write. I don't have one—I have fifteen. Then, when I focus on what I love, I discover that meeting each week and sharing and growing together is what I love. I love talking with these women about what lights them up. I learn how to connect to them . . . through story . . . through Zoom . . . during a pandemic. While everything else shuts down, we rediscover ourselves. And by writing and telling my stories, I connect with myself, and I fall in love with me.

It is exciting to know that what I see in them is in me too. I am proud of the woman who survived an abusive marriage and saved her son; the one who values family and friendship after being abandoned by her dad; the one who became healthy through healing, clean foods and movement in nature after being diagnosed with an incurable autoimmune disease. I am proud of the woman who built a successful career and then gave it up to follow her passion. I am proud of myself that I listened to my intuition and said "heck yes" to Maya, this community and myself.

And—I found my voice. I now follow my heart even when it doesn't seem practical. I believe and trust that the dots *will* connect in the future.

"I HAD to overcome my public speaking fear.

But how?

I began to lean into the fear."

Let Fear Be Your Guide

Jennifer Cavender

During my second year at a local community college, I was required to take a course that absolutely terrified me: public speaking.

Every written speech I turned in received a high score, but the delivery was agonizing.

As I would stand up from my chair and begin walking toward the stage, I would feel the pit in my stomach rise up to my throat. As I would reach the stage and look out at the sea of students, heat would rise through my chest and neck and turn my face a bright red. I'd look down at my note cards and begin speaking. My quivering voice would fail to project across the room and my knees would start to shake. Occasionally, I'd try to look up from my note cards. But it was useless. The parts of the speech that I had spent so much time memorizing would be gone, and I would fully read from my note cards. Just as I thought my body would explode from the stress, my time would end, and I would sheepishly walk off the stage to my seat.

That was my experience every time I was in front of a group of people.

During my third year in college, I transferred to a nearby university and joined an honors society for accounting students called Beta Alpha Psi (BAP). In BAP, I began to really learn about my chosen career and realized that public accounting was not just being in an office counting beans. Communication and presentation were extremely important. And the other students seemed to be *amazing* at them!

I quickly learned that the more visible students who held officer positions in BAP were pretty much guaranteed a job offer from a large accounting firm. And I wanted to be one of those students. But that meant I had to give a speech! And continue to speak in front of the organization every week!

I chose this career to have a stable job so . . . *I HAD to overcome my public speaking fear.*

But how?

I began to lean into the fear.

I ran for every student position I could. I volunteered for class presentations. I asked my pastor if I could read scripture in front of the church, and I did it as much and as often as I could!

I spent two years practicing public speaking. And by the time I graduated college, I had become president of BAP and learned to *love* being in front of an audience!

In my corporate accounting career, I became the strongest presenter in the entire firm!

My confidence when I speak publicly has set me apart in my career, and the impact I am able to have brings me so much joy.

In this, I learned the importance of moving through your fear because your greatest strength is just on the other side.

"It was like a switch was flipped and my entire world was infused with color."

Infuse Your Life with Color

Lesley Rosas

Have you ever stood on the brink of a decision knowing that it could change your entire future for better or worse?

Have you ever held back from pursuing your dreams for fear of what they might bring?

We are each just one decision away from altering our entire life!

Ten years ago, I made a decision that totally shifted the direction of my life when I left my emotionally and physically abusive husband on our twenty-fifth anniversary. Originally, I had not planned to leave that day. Married at 17, I had given him 25 years and 12 birth children. I was terrified every day of what could happen to the children if we left, and I knew what could happen if we stayed. "What ifs" were constantly cycling through my mind, and I knew it was up to me to live a life that would most protect my kids. So, I had stayed in the abuse for all those years believing the sacrifice would save them. Believing the lie that if I changed enough, I could shift my marriage.

On our anniversary, his abuse was particularly terrifying, and suddenly I knew I had one choice to make: Stay and he kills us or leave and he *may* find and kill us. That day, I made my decision to leave. Gathering the little children into my room and in whispers feigning delight, I told them, "I have a secret. We are going on an adventure, a vacation! It is our secret. Go pack your things and don't tell anyone."

We snuck away with only our clothes and a 10-person tent, driving our 15-passenger van across the USA, stopping only late at night at KOA camps for a brief sleep and staying on backroads whenever we could. After three days, we arrived in California where we lived at a camp—homeless for the next three months while I got a restraining order and custody of my kids. The day I was granted custody was a dream come true. Finally, I had a protective order and could keep my children safe.

Soon after that, we changed locations, and I rented us a house in the town where I had been born, raised and graduated from high school. Family members and new friends donated beds, pillows and kitchenware to set up our new household. And for the first time in their lives, my kids lived in a home where they did not have to fear for their lives. And for the first time in my life, I was free! I should have felt so happy, but I didn't. I felt stuck and frozen. I wondered who I was and where the girl I once was went, and I just wanted to be loved.

One day, I was walking down the main street, just putting one foot in front of the other, looking down at my black leather shoes and the skirt of my homemade Mennonite Cape dress. I knew this dress like it was a part of me. I'd sewn hundreds of them. The same pattern, the same dress every season and every year for the previous 17 years as a member of the Mennonite Church.

As I was walking, I thought to myself, "My life is drained of all of its color. My life is black and white." And in that thought and in that moment, I spied something colorful in the shop window. There, on display, were the cutest pair of red, lace-up Converse rubber boots. I stopped to admire them and thought, "But they're red, and I have not been allowed to wear red as a Mennonite . . . " followed by, "BUT THEY'RE RED, and I am no longer a Mennonite!" I walked into that shop and found that those boots were my exact size. The moment I put them on, it was like a switch was flipped and my entire world was infused with color.

Today, I am married to the love of my life. Together, we have raised a blended family of 17 and await the arrival of our fourteenth grandchild. I am living the dream of a safe, loving home and a joyful family. And now I have the privilege of inspiring other women around the world who desire to improve their lives.

I believe it takes just one decision to change your entire life.

"I realized I didn't cherish the idea of being with myself."

Your Greatest Love Lives Within You

Shannon Reinhard-Chapoy

Have you ever wanted to be loved by someone else so badly? Always looking for love outside yourself?

For years, this was my unspoken mission. I wanted a partner to love me and enjoy things we loved together. I so desperately wanted this love that I was doing courses, coaching and all sorts of work to find it.

Then one day, Maya asked me, "What would *you* love? What would a date with you look like?"

I thought, "A date with me?!! What does she mean? Why would I want to go on a date with me?"

I realized I didn't cherish the idea of being with myself on a date—a way to have fun with someone. I couldn't imagine having fun with myself.

I felt the pain of my own self-rejection. And I thought, "If I don't enjoy my own company or know the things I enjoy doing, how can I expect someone else to fulfill this for me?" It was an eye-opener!

To be honest, it was painful to realize that I didn't *know* what I truly loved to do on my own—because I'd been focused on pleasing other people and finding the ideal partner to give me the love I desired.

It was then that I started on my "what would I love" journey. I learned that I love taking walks on the beach, and I love beautiful food and I love Latin dancing. I just never realized I could enjoy these things on my own.

One day, I took myself out on a date to a beach restaurant. I ordered two amazing exotic appetizers: grilled artichokes and asparagus with a lemon cream sauce and seared sea scallops with a brandy citrus sauce. I doubt I would have ever ordered these if I was actually on a date because I'd be worried what my date thought. Then I had my favorite dessert: chocolate lava cake oozing out warm creamy sauce with berries on top. Yum! I didn't worry what anyone thought of me sitting alone or about the calories. It was amazing to order exactly what I wanted and enjoy every bite!

I noticed a couple in front of me looking so in love. And I felt so happy for them because I was finally feeling this love too. Inside myself!

After dinner, I went for a walk on the beach, listening to the waves and feeling their freshness and saltiness. I closed my eyes, and I took it all in. Then I went home and had a dance party for one . . . with Latin music. I danced like no one was watching, "Bailandoooo, bailando, bailandooo, bailando, na na na na na na . . . "

Eventually, I fell into the sofa, exhausted from enjoying my night on the beach, tasting all the exotic foods and dancing to my favorite music, completely satisfied with *my* date night.

I came to realize that I was looking for the greatest love outside myself. And I came to discover that my greatest love lives within me.

I believe that the greatest love for all of us lives within each one of us.

*"I faced death and fought for my life
just so I could share today—from the bottom of my
heart—how precious a gift Life is."*

Life, the Most Precious Gift of All

Marina Haralanova

Have you ever felt like life was fading away and you had to fight for it? I did! I fought, and I won!!!

It was 1986. At that time, I was living in my beautiful country, Bulgaria. A small piece of Earth's heaven filled with all of nature's gifts: golden sand beaches, green and majestic mountains, sunflower fields, vineyards, orchards and rose valleys. I remember vividly one bright summer day that I spent at my grandma's colorful garden in the villages. I was playing and swirling around, carried away by all that lovely place had to offer—flower aromas, buzzing bees and chirping birds.

All of a sudden, everything started blurring in front of my eyes. My cheerful squeals had become a desperate moan. I couldn't talk . . . I couldn't walk . . . I couldn't move.

And just like that, life was fading away from my little body.

Before I knew it, I was at the hospital, where I was diagnosed with a systemic infection caused by an insect bite. I suffered multiple organ failure and had a mere 10 percent chance of survival. My parents, who had just had my brother five days prior, were all torn apart because they were told that it was too late . . .

But was it really?

Though I knew little about life, faith, hope and destiny, the universe and God had different plans for me and my future. Contrary to the poor medical prognosis, a miracle had happened, and I started slowly recovering.

It wasn't too late after all! I was a fighter, and my soul was not quite ready to leave or give up.

Five months later, as I sat on the hospital bed waiting to go home, my favorite doctor of all, Dr. Stamboliiski—a tall man in a white hospital coat with a deep but warm voice—picked me up and brought me to the window. There, he said the words that became the mantra of my life: "You are just like these stars in the sky. Despite the clouds and the storms, they are always there shining and not giving up; just like you didn't. Your life will be full of endless possibilities. There will be ups and downs, but remember to keep shining and never give up."

And here I am, 34 years later, sharing the story of my life. I captured those words so deeply in my heart that they *became me* and propelled me to live life with passion no matter what I do. At such a young age, I faced death and fought for my life just so I could share today— from the bottom of my heart—how precious a gift Life is.

Twenty years ago, this deep desire to live life to the fullest brought me to the United States. Following my heart and dreams, I moved to this country of freedom in a journey of self-discovery. A few years after my arrival, my infinite love for living a healthy and vital life naturally brought me to nursing. That was my way to give back, to serve and express my gratitude.

Along the way, I was blessed to meet my amazing husband. And almost three years ago, we started a family when I gave the gift of life by giving birth to my beautiful daughter. The path of a young immigrant was not always the easiest, but it was my path, my love story and my journey of becoming, unbecoming and always growing.

I choose today and forever to love Life—that most precious gift of all—and live it with passion no matter the obstacles along the way! I will be forever grateful that I was given a second chance so I could continue enjoying this beautiful journey of Life, spread my message and help others embrace and live it!

"My life was killing me. I had to start living."

It's Never Too Late
Janet Annand

Have you ever asked yourself, "Is there more to life than this?"

At age 58, my days were very long. I woke up between 3:00 am and 4:30 am to begin work at 5:00 am. When I was done with work at 1:00 pm, I'd start housework, laundry, yardwork, errands, cooking dinner and taking care of my elderly mother. Around midnight, after cleaning the kitchen, I would finally crawl into bed. A few hours later, I'd get up and repeat the same routine. Day . . . after . . . day. When my 2-year-old grandson visited, he would run over on his little legs to hug me. I would return his hug, then go back to what I was doing—my mind was so focused on what I needed to do that I couldn't appreciate those precious moments.

Then I had five car accidents in 14 months. My friend Liz kept telling me, "The universe is sending you a message; you need to listen." I laughed about it but kept going. After the last accident, I realized she was right. I couldn't do it anymore. My life was killing me. I had to start living.

But where to start? How would I make a change?

One day, I received an email for a women's retreat in Vail. Without thinking, I signed up. Then I panicked! I had *never* spent $3000 for anything and certainly not on myself. I was terrified. I wanted to change my mind so many times. But I had spent so much on it. There must have been a reason for that. My heart told me it was time to put myself first.

The retreat was amazing! I even climbed a mountain. And when I stood on the top of that mountain, I believed I could do anything!

So I have! Since then, I have done everything my heart says "yes" to.

I became a Reiki practitioner.
I studied singing bowl therapy.
I made a native drum.
I studied pranic healing.
I experienced a temazcal (sweat lodge) in Mexico.

Then at age 61, I signed up for a Wim Hof class, which included immersing myself in a plastic tub full of water and ice for two minutes! I was older than anyone there by at least 20 years. Yikes! What was I doing?! As I waited in line watching the others, and thinking I was crazy, I thought, "Bullshit . . . I *can* do this!" And I did. It was sooo cold! The longest two minutes of my life! But what a feeling of exhilaration and accomplishment when I finished!

After that, I got a tattoo of the word "Bullshit" on my wrist to remind me I can do anything at any age! All the stories about what I should do or shouldn't do are just that—bullshit!

Now I know that we are meant to enjoy life. We aren't meant to be so bogged down by all the to-dos that we're blinded to that truth.

My grandson, at age 6, hugged me goodbye one day and said, "I could hug you forever." And recently, when I was making him lunch, he randomly walked over to me and said, "Grandma, your hugs are really special because every time you hug me I feel so much better."

I realized from the simple words of a 6-year-old how much of what I have learned to love and cherish I nearly missed. I have a dream now to travel the world and teach people the joy, beauty and warmth of a hug. I never would have imagined at age 58 that I would be living and loving my life the way I do!

I believe life is meant to be an adventure to enjoy! The big parts and the small things, even the meaning in a simple hug! It's never too late to start!

"They did need a Hispanic woman's voice on campus. Specifically, la voz de Patricia Lucero."

Live the Wisdom of Your Intuition
Patricia Lucero

Have you ever known and felt something so deeply you can't imagine another possibility? An undeniable message revealing itself to you in a way only you recognize. Perhaps it's the flutter of butterfly wings in your stomach or goosebumps on your arms.

For me it's a quiet whisper, like the moment I first set foot on the beautiful tree-lined campus of the University of Texas at Austin. It was the summer of 1981, and I was *awestruck*. Without warning, a voice inside me said, "You're home Patricia. Loneliness doesn't live here. This school and town are your sanctuary where you will find the love and happiness you deserve. This is where you belong." I had no reason to believe this voice, but somehow I knew to trust it. From that day forward, I had one goal: receive my acceptance letter to UT and with it, my freedom.

The next seven years were full of highs and lows, in school and at home. I passed my classes and took the SAT. The only thing left to do was wait for the letter that said, "Welcome! You're a Longhorn!" The letter that would answer my seven-year prayer.

Fast forward to my senior year. As I pulled into our driveway after school, I saw my mom standing in the garage waving an envelope. "Is today the day I finally get my answer?" The envelope was so plain and thin; it both baffled and scared me. More than a "yes" or "no" was in that envelope. I reached for it while holding my breath and steeled myself for the words I was about to read. What would I do if this letter was a rejection of seven years of hard work and dreaming? You see, UT was the *only* school I applied to.

As I was about to remove the letter from the envelope, my mom blurted out, "*Te aceptaron. Abrí tu sobre. Tuve que saber.*" "You got in. I opened your letter. I had to know."

I felt so confused because I was the happiest and most relieved I'd ever been, and yet I was so incredibly angry. I'd finally received the answer to my many prayers, and my mom had stolen my life-changing moment.

Later that evening, I was excited to share the news with my father. I hoped it would go better than with my mom. Instead, he responded, "You're probably a quota. You're a woman and Hispanic." In that moment, 17 years of his messaging sunk in. I'm a woman. I'm less than. I knew my father could be unkind in his opinions of women, but I never thought he was talking about me, his own daughter. I was devastated.

Despite the profound anger and sadness of that day, the voice that I first heard as a child said, "Keep going, Patricia. Keep fighting for yourself."

My father's words made me feel like a charity case for many years despite knowing I earned my grades with hard work and dedication. But what he said was actually true about UT needing me. They *did* need a Hispanic woman's voice on campus. Specifically, *la voz de Patricia Lucero.*

In 1992, with diploma in hand and pride in my heart, I walked across the stage and graduated from UT. And so did that 11-year-old girl who had faith her inner voice was guiding her toward happiness. The girl who became the woman whose intuition guides her everyday to speak her truth out loud.

Our intuition, our inner voice, *is* truth. She is our life's compass. Be still and listen for her wisdom. Give her the freedom to speak through you. Give her the opportunity to speak out loud the knowledge within you. You are a marvelous person deserving to be heard.

"That moment became the strongest foundation I ever planted my feet on."

The *Unstuckable* You
Kristin Zako

On September 27, 2003, the night of my wedding, I woke up in the ICU. I opened my eyes and saw my wedding dress hanging in the doorway. I had almost died from type 1 diabetes.

It was the beginning of 12 years of hurt.

The next year, I learned that my husband was a compulsive gambler and addicted to painkillers. I almost lost everything. How did I not know? I felt stupid and betrayed! It felt like I shared my bed with a stranger.

I chose to leave that marriage.

After that, I experienced heart palpitations and extreme anxiety. I was diagnosed with Graves' disease. I had two autoimmune diseases. I couldn't sleep, I had no energy and weight loss was a challenge.

A few years later, my step-nephew Danny was killed in the Chardon High School shooting.

My niece gave birth to a beautiful baby boy. Sixteen days later, the father broke both of the baby's legs.

Three months after that, my phone rang. It was my sister. My 26-year-old nephew, Nick, was killed in a car accident.

I threw the phone. I was done.

I don't have children, so my nieces and nephews are my kids. When Nick died, it felt like I lost my own son. My world was shattered.

There were days I couldn't get out of bed. I would wake up and feel the weight of an elephant on my body. And if I did get out of bed, I carried the weight of the hurt from the last 12 years. I was stuck in my pain. I couldn't put a grocery list together let alone make a meal, so I ate junk. My blood sugar was out of control, and I didn't care.

One evening, as I drove home from work, the hurt was so unbearable that I could hardly breathe. I thought:

Fuck it!
Jerk the wheel.
Go off the bridge.
Make it all stop.

That moment became the strongest foundation I ever planted my feet on.

I realized I needed help.
I couldn't do it alone.
I didn't want to stay stuck anymore.
I wanted to make serious changes.
I didn't want to be the reason for my family to suffer yet another loss.
And I knew I was meant for more.

I hired a coach that offered the structure and support I needed. I joined communities to keep the momentum going and dove into self-education. I attended retreats and connected with beautiful souls on a similar path. I committed to one year of walking in nature for at least 10 minutes every day—rain, snow or shine. *No excuses!*

It's now been more than two years since I made that commitment, and it's changed my life forever. Connecting nature and motion consistently has been my ultimate healer. Now, my mind is clear, and the elephant is off my chest. My energy is high, I sleep great, my blood sugar is stable, the Graves' disease is under control and I feel stronger than I did when I was in my 20s. And I am married to the most incredible man for love, life and adventure.

I am so grateful for being alive and having the ability to show others that there is hope and healing after hurt. I believe that every single one of us is *unstuckable!*

"That made me so happy, not just because everyone else had fun—that was important—but that I did too."

The Gift of a Little Sparkle
Christine Burke

Have you ever thought: "It has been so long since I had real fun"?

I remember one day last August I had such a thought.

Every morning, I set an intention for my day as it begins. Sitting in bed that particular Sunday, I thought about my intention. "*Have fun*" popped right up in my mind. As I sat with those words—*have fun*—I wasn't really making complete sense of them.

A commanding voice in my head was saying, "*YOU: have fun*" almost as if I had to convince myself. A part of me said, "I know you're going to make sure everyone else has fun, but this is about *you . . . having . . . fun.*"

As I sat there with those words—*have fun*—I *really* felt confused.

I went over to the closet to get dressed; we were going to play mini golf that day, which we all love.

The message was still blaring: "You have fun, Christine. YOU!"

So I looked at my clothes in my closet and thought, "Maybe fun is dressing up?" No, that wasn't it. I wanted to wear my jean shorts and a t-shirt.

I then went to grab my shoes, and when I looked down, I noticed flat shoes with sparkles, like bedazzled sparkly gems, that I bought to wear at weddings—the "look good/feel good" kind.

For some reason, my attention was drawn to those shoes. It was like they wanted to be worn . . . "We are sparkly and sparkles are fun."

I put the shoes on my feet, and I turned around to my 6-year-old daughter, Juliana, who said, "What are you doing? Are you wearing those shoes?"

"Yes."

"But we are going mini golfing."

"I know, and I am having fun today, and these shoes are fun."

"Ok, Mom. Are you changing your clothes because those are fancy shoes?"

"Nope. I am not."

"Ok, Mom. Then let's go!"

And off we went.

On the third hole, I got a hole in one—the first of us to make one that day! I couldn't contain myself; I jumped up and down and danced all around, while in my head singing, "You can do the winner dance!"

We all laughed, and my children quickly moved on to the next hole to get their opportunity for a hole in one . . . and a winner dance.

We all did it that day.

As we drove home from miniature golf and dinner, laughter filled the car, and I felt so alive. I could not remember the last time we all felt so alive. My son, Jacob, said, "That was fun . . . today was a lot of fun." That made me so happy, not just because everyone else had fun—that was important—but that I did too, and that we all did together.

Back home, as I went to take my shoes off, I paused. For a moment I got really sad, like maybe my fun was only when I wore my sparkly shoes.

And then I remembered my sparkly shoes were simply a reminder of the fun that already existed *within me*.

PART TWO

Living Legacy

"How could I show her what was truly possible for her dreams when I was not fulfilling my own?"

Love Is Leading the Way
Kate Butler

When my first child was born and the nurse placed her on my chest, she looked directly into my eyes, and we were locked in love. I had never experienced anything like it before in my life. All the doctors and nurses that were in and out of our room over those three days commented on it. They noted how aware she was for a newborn, and how she would not break her gaze with me no matter where she was in the room, who was holding her or what was going on. We locked in our bond the moment our eyes met, and it was an unparalleled love.

The moment Bella was born, something was born inside me as well.

Each time I gazed upon this child, my heart exploded with possibility. I could see dreams coming alive for her. I could see what she was capable of and all that she was meant to do here.

I made it my mission to show her what was possible.

During our bedtime stories, I made up new endings to her books to illustrate the great big world and all that she could do, be, have, create and fulfill.

Yet, one night, as I rewrote the ending to her bedtime story, I began to weep.

How could I show her what was truly possible for her dreams when I was not fulfilling my own?

I had to be better and do better. If I could not find a way inside to do it for me, then I had to dig deeper and find a way to do it for *her*.

That night, the magic that was born inside me the day Bella was born was reignited, and the flame came back fierce.

Bella had given me the gift of love. Though I could not do it for myself, I could show up and do it for her. I could dig deep, pick myself up and fight against the odds to show her what it looked like to follow big dreams.

So, I walked away from the company I had built up from the ground up. I could have stayed there forever and made plenty of money. I would have been "just fine." The company employed people from all over the country, and there was a time I took great pride in that. But I was settling. I was emotionally and spiritually bankrupt, and no amount of money could fill that void. "Just fine" was no longer good enough.

I sold my company and started to dream again. My spiritual path immediately opened up, and, as fate would have it, I reunited with a friend who invited me to a meditation retreat. It was a four-day immersion to get back in touch with my higher self. There, my life's purpose began to unfold, and, for the first time in years, I felt inspired by something within me, and not something or someone external. This burning desire to create more and step into more was coming from my soul, and I was ready to listen and leap.

This path led me to publish my first children's book. I then went on to write additional books with both of my daughters. We now travel and share our books and messages all over the world, and we follow and fulfill our dreams together.

I may not have had the belief in myself at the time, but I allowed the belief I had in my daughter and my desire to show her the way to pull me through. I couldn't let her down. My love for her was greater than the doubt I had in myself. My love for her lit the way, and it led me to fulfill a life of love for myself as well.

Love spoke through my daughter's eyes on the day she was born.
Love spoke through dreams I had for her.
Love spoke through the new fairytale endings I created in our bedtime stories.
Love spoke through the belief I had in my daughter that I borrowed for myself.
Love spoke through finally showing up in my passion.
Love spoke through that passion leading to our family purpose.
Love speaks each day through our books and work.
Love speaks when readers share that their lives are changed.
Love speaks in magnificent ways, and I am so grateful for all the ways it speaks to us, through us and for us.

Love is leading the way.

"I had to trust. I had to trust in the unfolding."

The Life List
Colleen Low

My son, Carter, has always been one of the greatest loves of my life. He loves to play, have fun and go on adventures. He loves playing all sorts of games—from Monopoly to pickleball.

When Carter was 18, right after graduating from high school, he served on a mission for our church. After about 14 months, he was sent home because he was having pain in his chest and back. He had lost a lot of weight, was coughing up blood and was taking pain medicine to get through the days.

After many tests, we learned that Carter had an aggressive cancer, large B-cell lymphoma, that had spread through his body with 100 percent coverage in his lungs and kidneys. Carter began high doses of chemo and immunotherapy immediately.

One day, my husband, John, and I were at the Anaheim Convention Center attending a Keller Williams convention. I had a feeling something was not right with Carter. We headed to the hospital and got off the elevator on the fifth floor. As we made our way down the hall to room 533, I noticed Carter's door was open. He never had his door open. My body immediately tensed, and I started to panic.

As we walked into Carter's room, four nurses surrounded his bed. One nurse hand-pumped medicine into him. Another nurse took over.

"What is going on?" I asked the charge nurse.

"Carter has klebsiella, streptococcus and hypertension. We're trying to get him stable," he replied.

My panic rose. I turned to God and started to scream in my head, "Why? Why would you do this? Why are you trying to take my son from me?" I heard and felt a voice that said, "He's just on loan to you. You are telling me what to do." I thought, "Oh my gosh, I *am* telling God what to do." I realized then I had to trust. I had to trust in the unfolding. I had to trust in God.

From that moment, everything moved in slow motion. They pumped four liters of bolus into Carter and sent him to the pediatric intensive care unit. We followed.

On the elevator ride up, I had a feeling that Carter and I should plan his dream vacation. When I got to his room, I sat next to him and asked, "Carter, if you could go anywhere in the world, where would you go? What would you do?" He said, "I would love to go to Italy— to Rome, Venice and the Amalfi Coast."

I wrote down everything he wanted to do. We planned out the entire trip, even including an Eastern Mediterranean cruise. We were so thrilled . . . amidst the chemo and the therapy treatments, we had an incredible adventure to look forward to.

All that planning tired Carter out, and he fell asleep. My heart started to race. I realized that we don't always have tomorrow. I also needed to live my dreams today. So, I pulled out my journal and wrote down everything I want to make sure I do.

Learn to paddleboard.
Have no regrets.
Become a best-selling author.
Visit Montana and buy a Montana lake house.
Create an inspirational podcast to help others reach their potential.
Make appreciation, intention and delegation journals to sell.
Go on annual family trips.
Wear fun clothes.
Become a top real estate agent for Keller Williams.
Donate $100,000 annually to help kids with cancer or addiction.
Become a motivational/inspirational speaker.
Own multiple rental properties.
Create a home yoga studio.
Spread love and light everywhere I go.
Take a family cruise to Alaska.
Hike Machu Picchu.
Serve a mission.
Have money to help people, not just wish I could help.

Carter is 23 now. We went on that magical trip to the Amalfi Coast . . . and we enjoyed every second of it. Carter is now attending university, working and killing it on the pickleball courts.

I too am doing all the things on my list. I learned to paddleboard and love it! I visited Montana. I'm a top-rated real estate agent for Keller Williams, and I am about to start my new podcast, Born to be Brave.

My mission is to remind people that this is not your practice life. Do what you love, now. You don't know if you have tomorrow, but you do have today. So, get started on *your* list!

"I made a promise to myself 'to choose happiness no matter what' because choosing creates possibilities."

Happily Ever Cyber
Sandra Estok

I was 11 years old, growing up in Venezuela, when my mom and I were evicted. The only place we could afford to pay rent was a "shack" with no running water and no bathroom. One day, after I was brutally bullied, I made a promise to myself "*to choose happiness no matter what*" because choosing creates possibilities.

I built a successful career in Information Technology, and, in 2005, my job relocated my husband and I from Venezuela to the Midwest of the USA. Oh, that weather!

After I survived our first winter, I went to visit my mom. On my return flight, as we landed in Miami, the pilot announced: "Folks, please cooperate; Homeland Security agents are boarding the plane."

I handed them my passport with my work visa. The next thing I knew, I was the one being marched off the plane and thrown into a room—yes, that room!

I wasn't allowed to make any phone calls. I didn't know what was happening! My husband was waiting for me in Chicago. And I was about to miss my connecting flight.

Ten hours later, I was handed back my passport.

"Revoked?"

We rushed back to Venezuela where I was trying to get a new visa with my former employer's attorney's help.

During the interview, the officials kept asking: "Why were you in China? Who do you know in China? Who is your contact?"

I didn't know what they were talking about. I'd never been to China.

But, somehow, a Cybermonster—using my identity—had been smuggling women into the US.

I convinced them that I was not a smuggler! I got my new visa, and everything seemed ok.

Two weeks later, when I returned from a trip to Europe, I got off the plane . . . and at passport control, I was marched right back into that room!

For the next six years of my life, I had to prove that I was the real me . . . over and over . . . every time I traveled. When I googled my name, everything was in Chinese. And can you believe nobody wanted to travel with me?! Not even my own husband!

Thankfully, I became a US citizen, and with my new passport and name, my travel issues went away. Shortly thereafter, I said "Yes" to a new career in the cybersecurity field. Finally, I understood why, what and how identity theft and cybercrime happens, as well as what to do and what not to do.

I've helped numerous public and private organizations, including Fortune 500 companies, develop and implement strong defenses against cybercrime.

In 2018, remembering once again my promise to myself to "choose happiness" and take action for the changes I wanted to see in my life and in this cyber world, I founded my own company, Way2Protect®. Identity theft and cybercrime can happen to anyone, but it doesn't have to happen to you, your family or business.

My mission is to change the way we perceive this cyber world so we can have Peace of Mind Online™. I believe you can become cyber savvy, take charge of your cybersafety and live Happily Ever Cyber ™!

"Even though I walked this path before with my mom, my path could be different."

Miracles and Lab Coats
Lena Winslow

It was early summer morning in a large hospital room overlooking a lake in Orlando, Florida. I was 18 years old, and my mom, Tatyana, was in a morphine-induced coma to manage her pain from cancer. She hadn't responded to anything for over a week.

Several weeks prior, Dr. M sat us down and told me and my mom, a 47-year-old Russian medical doctor, that her breast cancer had progressed. "There is nothing else we can do," she said. I translated the conversation into Russian for my mom. It seemed so clinical. These two amazing, strong women in lab coats were speaking about the end of life. There were no tears. There was no emotion. Just the facts. I wondered, "Are they just being strong for me? Does it seem so sterile because they are doctors, or is it because I am sitting here in front of them?"

I believed in miracles. I always did.
"It's not over," my soul whispered. "It never is."

I witnessed my mother's brilliant mind and never-ending drive to help others over a lifetime. She was one of the first women in Azerbaijan to graduate medical school. She became a pediatrician, cardiologist, sports medicine specialist and neurologist. She took care of everyone else while her own body started to fade away.

I watched her transition from doctor to patient.

Her mind drifted into a chemo fog, and her soul froze in silence, unable to share what was about to happen. Finally, I had the guts to say, albeit timidly, "Mom, *they* say you are leaving me." She responded, "Never. I will always be with you and your sister."

We never spoke of it again.

I could tell she didn't want to return to the subject. A few days later, she slowly and silently slipped into a coma—her body and mind got quiet, still and peaceful. Monitors and morphine pumps chirped and dripped round the clock, and her nurse, sweet Peggy, worked every night shift.

Stepping out of the bathroom that morning, I went to my mom and took her hand in mine. Suddenly, her hand felt cold—a cold I never felt before. I repeated her words over and over: "I will always be with you and your sister." I prayed for a miracle.

Twenty years later, when I was 38 years old, my husband, Dave, and I drove three hours to visit a familiar face—Dr. M.

I was still waiting for a miracle.

The exam room door opened. That fierce mind already analyzed all the records I sent over, and the medical history she wrote up on me after this visit was the best I have ever seen. This time, however, Dr. M was not so clinical. Her eyes looked moist as she told me, "Her story is not your story."

I saw her heart and soul in her eyes; she was a whole different oncologist—the fearless kind. I had always trusted her mind. That day, I also trusted her soul when she told me my path was different from my mother's 20 years ago.

I believed her. I believed that even though I walked this path before with my mom, my path could be different. And it was. I combined conventional medicine with integrative holistic health principles.

I had a double mastectomy.
I had reconstructive surgery.
I fasted.
I used acupuncture.
I had chemotherapy.
I exercised.
I practiced mindfulness.
I went on walks in nature.
And most of all, I believed.

That was three years ago. Today, I am completely in the clear with no cancer indicators. I get to be the mom and wife that I love to be with my three kids and my husband.

And I finally found my miracle.

Now, I guide professionals and caregivers to connect amazing minds with equally amazing souls living in healthy bodies.

I believe that there is an intersection between the mind, the body, the soul and medicine. And when we use an integrative approach, all things are possible, and miracles happen.

"There was, in fact, an Army of Angels helping, guiding and protecting me through the darkest times."

Army of Angels
Sammy Taggett

The summer of 2015 in Denver was crazy. Pot was legal, and the dance music scene had exploded. I was a DJ in one of the biggest little party towns in Colorado. I performed in all the best hot spots and even performed on the main stage at Red Rocks, opening for Global Dance Fest with Empire of the Sun, Kid Cudi, Kaskade and Skrillex! It was weekend after weekend of debauchery—no one charged me for drinks, and I could always find drugs anywhere in the city.

On the outside looking in, you would think I was on top of the world. But underneath my larger than life persona was a scared and confused child running from party to party looking for the next quick fix. I had a growing substance problem, a reckless business and a life built on a house of cards as I tried desperately to find my place in a scene that was full of empty promises.

Things had to change, and I knew it.

Despite my crazy party streak, I had one consistent belief: I knew I was destined for bigger things. When I was a baby, I was adopted from an orphanage in the Philippines and brought to Colorado. I always had a dream of going back to the Philippines to find my roots and save all the kids. Even in the party throngs, I would share my vision to anyone that would listen about this dream in hopes that they might somehow help get me there.

Enter my dear friend Jason. Jason also had a dream of going to the Philippines to deliver clean drinking water systems to people in the remote jungles. He planned to go later that year. Once he heard my vision he said, "You have to come with us!"

"I AM TOTALLY IN!" I said.

It was decided. I felt the world shift underneath me.

Could I actually just do this?

"You *have* to do this; you are *called* to do this!" I said to myself.

The next few weeks were a flurry of excitement and hard work as we assembled our team—Jason, me, Norm, Derek and Brandi. We became fast friends as we worked to raise money for the clean water initiative and map out our journey. I even found out that Brandi and I were adopted at the same time from the same orphanage!

Before my flight, I called my parents; I was both excited and nervous for the adventure.

"You know mom, we're going to the very place I was adopted from; how wild would that be if I actually met my biological mom?" I said as an afterthought.

There was silence on the other end of the phone. It was deafening. It seemed like a couple of minutes before my mom even responded.

Did I say something wrong?
Did I hurt my mother's feelings?

There was a new tone in her voice. I could feel the gravity of it. I stopped everything I was doing.

"You need to look at the folder we gave you a while back. Did you look at those papers? Did you read what was in that folder?" she asked. I remembered when she gave me the papers. I brushed them aside, barely even looking at them.

"I'll look at them before I leave! Promise." I said, trying to brush it off again.

"No, Samuel John. You need to look through those papers. There are some things you need to know before you leave, and you need to go through them by yourself." She was rarely this forceful. My heart started to race.

"Ok ok, I will, I promise." As I ended the call, I reached for the folder. My heart started pounding a little harder.

I laid the contents of the folder out on the table.

An old photo of me with sores all over my body.
A letter from my parents written to their son to be.
A certificate from the Republika ng (of) The Philippines.

My heart started pounding louder; my hands were sweaty. How had I never read through this?

The writing was worn and old; I could see indentations from the typewriter. The paper was almost completely translucent and so delicate that I almost tore it just laying it on the table.

I read the following:

"... *hearing held on December 3rd, 1976 ... evidence produced minor was born on April 14th, at Balintawak, Quezon City; That on that same date, the mother placed the subject child in a shoebox and was about to commit infanticide when apprehended ...*"

What? I read it again: *"mother placed the subject child in a shoebox and was about to commit infancticide."*

My heart was pounding so loud now, I only heard the rush of blood over my eardrums. The room spun. I was dizzy.

I was put in a shoebox.
I was placed in a dumpster.
I WAS BEING THROWN AWAY.

Silence overtook me. I couldn't hear anything; it was as if the air had been sucked completely out of the room. No more pounding heart, no more ambient sounds, no more sound at all. The silence was deafening.

Then, as if from a distance, I heard it ... it was faint, but I heard it.

Drip.
Drip.
Drip.
Drip.

Where was that coming from? Something was spilling as if someone had tipped a drink on the table!

Oh no! The papers! I didn't want whatever was dripping to ruin them. I looked around to see if anything had spilled on the floor.

I was on the floor.

"How did I get here?" I wondered.

The dripping continued. What was it!? I looked down at the documents, and I finally spotted the drops that had made a small pool on the worn-out print. I rushed to dry the papers, and I realized that the drops were mine. My tears had been streaming down my face and dripping onto the floor.

Drip.
Drip.
Drip.

For the first time in years, I was crying.

It hit me—a wave of guilt, shame and embarrassment. How could I have been so reckless with this life, with these opportunities? My chest heaved as I sobbed, and I laid back down on the floor. Everything was numb. I felt completely broken.

Then, just as suddenly as it began, it stopped. I bolted upright as if someone tied a string to my back.

I had a mission.
I was headed back to my homeland.
I had a plane to catch!

I closed my eyes and took a huge breath of fresh air. A tide turned in me that night, and once the shame and guilt subsided, a new seed took root: the idea that there was, in fact, an Army of Angels helping, guiding and protecting me through the darkest times. I knew then that life was not meant to be thrown away.

To feel and acknowledge the truth was the first step.

Two souls created me.
My mother set me free.
Two police officers rescued me.
The beautiful angels at the orphanage cared for me.
My angel parents adopted me.
Hundreds of people supported me to get to Colorado to begin a new, incredible life.

I had an Army of Angels supporting me.

I realized that had it not been for that Army of Angels, I might not be here.

From the time we arrived in the Philippines, we set forth to do amazing things. We travelled as a team deep into the jungles. We delivered 90 water filters and were met with the most beautiful smiles.

We found the orphanage where Brandi and I were protected and cared for until we made our way to our families in Colorado.

I still love music and being a DJ. But how I perform and cultivate music changed that day I found myself on the floor. I now recognize the gift of life that I was given. I've started to perform more for the people that I know are angels here on earth—the coaches and sages of our day who perform miracles as they help to support the human race.

I'm blessed to use my unique talents and skills in music and connection to bond tribes around the world as we lift and raise the vibration both on and off the dance floor.

Lastly, and most importantly, I was able to connect with my orphanage and work with them to co-create a better environment by helping to create unique learning environments and provide supplies so that the children of tomorrow have a safer home today.

Here's to finding your Army of Angels.

PART THREE

Born For This

"I was feeling again . . .
and the pain was excruciating."

Fearless Feelings

Kerry Norton

"Gonna love her."

"Who are you talking about," I said.

"Our daughter. I'm gonna really love her."

This was the vision Christoph shared with me the morning after our first kiss. It was magical. We picnicked in the moonlight and skinny-dipped in the lake.

"I accept you with all the consequences," he said.

Six months earlier, I burst through the door of a small coffee shop in central Switzerland, desperate for a wee. On my return from the loo, I noticed a man sitting at the other side of the bar reading a book. He looked up and smiled. Embarrassed, I looked away, ordered my coffee and started scrolling through social media on my phone.

Like. Like. Love. Comment. Happy face emoji . . .

I stopped for a moment, wondering what to post. A swell of emotion rose up inside me, and I quickly washed it down with a gulp of hot coffee and went back to scrolling.

That was the first time I had ventured down into the valley from our new home in the mountains. I had to take our beloved dog Maggie to the vet. She had a lump, and we were fearful that her cancer had returned. Moving to Switzerland was our big adventure—a way to forget all the heartache, loss and bitterness of the past decade. With our son about to turn 4, it was the perfect time to get away from it all.

It was idyllic, living on a ski resort in the Swiss Alps. I was busy doing all the things to show just how happy I was—posting pictures of the epic expanse that was the view from my yoga mat, posing my breakfast and adding heavy filters to my selfies. I didn't share the daily use of marijuana and the dozen or so empty wine bottles I was dropping off for recycling every week.

It was still dark when I left the apartment with Maggie that morning. It was freezing, and heavy snowfall from the night before made the walk to the mountain train slow. I checked the time on my phone. We were late! I started to run, but with every step, I fell deeper and deeper into the snow. All I could think was, "I cannot miss this train. I have to make everything ok."

I was exhausted and frantic, crawling on my hands and knees across the ice. I prayed, "Please help me. Please help us. I cannot do this on my own."

Back in the coffee shop, the man was getting ready to leave, yet something stopped him. "What's that for, a book you're reading?" he said.

To my surprise, I was open, and, like old friends, we talked for hours. He told me that his name was Christoph; he lived in the mountains with his two teenage children; he was an unemployed computer programmer and a healer.

After that day, something inside me changed. I stopped smoking and I stopped drinking. Creativity returned, and I began writing and dreaming. I was feeling again . . . and the pain was excruciating. I felt awful. My gut was twisted and my soul ached. I couldn't eat; I couldn't sleep. I resisted it, but I could no longer ignore all that was hurting, all that was missing.

Months went by, and finally, I admitted it—I had fallen in love. My feelings would cost me everything: my marriage, our family together, the home we built and many friends. I was terrified.

Four years on, one divorce, a fearless 3-year-old daughter and a contented baby boy later, Christoph and I are now a family of seven. I would not change it—not the pain and the shame of it all—for the world.

I believe that your most joyful destiny lives on the other side of your deepest despair. There is no denying it: choosing to feel is frightening. But, if we have the courage to trust in life, and stop numbing the pain and suppressing the uncomfortable emotions, who knows what love, passion and abundance wait for us on the other side?

"Living is my adventure,
and I am off those damn sidelines!"

Sidelines No More
Linda Scherer

It was June 7, 1958, and I was at a monthly Family Circle meeting at my uncle's house. Family was arriving and gathering in the basement. There were small groups of people chatting; I was in one corner of the room with my mom, dad and my two older brothers, Gary and Rickie. One of my cousins came over and said hello to everyone; then he looked at me and said, "Hi Linda, cat still got your tongue?" Before I could utter a single word, my mother quickly jumped in with a chuckle, "No, Linda's just quiet." I turned red with embarrassment, and I wanted to cry and disappear into thin air! Instead, I said nothing and just hid behind my mother, clutching her leg.

For years after that, I sat on the sidelines of life. I was afraid that speaking up would lead to judgment, laughter and ridicule. So, I stayed silent. I wouldn't share my thoughts or opinions in my career, at school or in my marriage. People called me "the quiet one" or "the enigma" because I would never share.

I thought to myself:

Stay low key. Don't stand out. Just be invisible. Try to fit in.
If you stay quiet, no one will laugh at you or judge you.
Don't say anything stupid.

Those thoughts served me well for a while. I worked for AT&T for 25 years and then another 12 years with Cigna Healthcare. I got promoted to HR Director and earned over six figures. But no matter how many times I got promoted or how many fancy titles I received, I still felt that I didn't *really* matter. I was just the "quiet enigma" that everyone would make fun of if I showed who I really was.

A voice inside of me started to awaken . . . to whisper:

You are more than this, Linda.

I longed to be more than this quiet woman who had no thoughts and no opinions. Deep down, I knew that wasn't truly me. I was *more* than that. I had to be. The life I was living . . . wasn't really living. It was merely existing.

Years later, after my husband, Bill, passed away, I was at the doctor's office filling out forms for my annual visit. I had to place a checkmark in the box to show whether I was single, married or a widow. I paused at the box for "widow." Tears welled up in my eyes; blood rushed to my face; my heart beat out of my chest. I felt nauseated, and then all the blood seemed to drain from my body. I wanted to scream, "I don't want this . . . This is *not* who I choose to be!"

The quiet one.
The enigma.
And now, the widow?!

"Noooooooo," I thought. "I can't just be a widow. That can't be all! There has to be more. I know I am *more*!"

When someone passes, people often say, "Start living; each day is precious; we don't know how much time we have." But it's only a matter of time before people sink back into regular patterns of living on the sidelines again, letting life pass by. I experienced this fleeting feeling after friends and loved ones passed away. But after Bill passed away, something shifted in me. I thought to myself, "Linda, it's time."

It's time to get off the sidelines.
Time to come alive.
Time to share your voice.
Time to speak up.
It is your time to be who you were born to be.

So I made a decision that day to get off those damn sidelines. I didn't exactly know what to do or how to do it. But I leaned in every time I heard that little voice that said there was *more*. That voice nudged me to join groups, speak my heart and mind and do things that, up until then, I wouldn't have done. I joined a coaching group with beautiful women who were all sharing their hearts with the world, and I started to share mine.

Now, at 69 years old, living is my adventure, and I am off those damn sidelines! I am no longer the quiet one, although I might still be an enigma ;-) You never know what I am up to these days!

I recently relocated from Arizona to Florida; I hiked up the Grand Canyon; I became a consultant for natural, clean and fresh skincare products. I have a coaching group called Live Your Best Life with Linda. And I have a column in a local monthly magazine with healthy recipes that goes to over 1100 homes!

I believe that death is more common than life. Everyone dies, but not everyone lives. So, get off those sidelines, and I will meet you on the field of life!

"I knew if people started treating me differently—
like I had a death sentence—
then I was going to die."

The Choice to Be Alive

Kathy Sweeney

It should have been a Monday like any other Monday. I was picking up groceries for dinner. But this particular Monday, I was also waiting for a phone call as I mindlessly pushed my grocery cart through the aisles.

Ring . . . Ring . . .

I immediately saw the vision of being on the ultrasound table just three days before:

I am going to pass out.
I feel so sick. "How can this be happening?"
They lay a cold towel over my brow and continue the ultrasound.
The radiologist says, "This looks suspicious." *I hate that word.*
"It's most likely cancer."
"What?" *I think.* "Don't they need a biopsy to confirm before they say something like that?"

I'm catapulted back to the grocery store. In the middle of the aisle,

I picked up the phone. It was the radiologist: "Mrs. Sweeney, the biopsy confirms that it is breast cancer." I thought, "Wait, what? I'm in a grocery store. I've got a cart full of food. Aren't we supposed to have an appointment to tell me bad news? And aren't I supposed to have my husband there with me?"

I left my cart full of groceries in the store.

Somehow, I made it home.

From that point, everything felt like a blur—being shuffled from one appointment to the next, enduring test after test. My right breast was unrecognizable, all battered and bruised, a constant reminder of what was beneath the surface.

A week later, I stood in the middle of a room at the plastic surgeon's office. I was naked with nothing more than a paper napkin covering up my privates while a photographer, a stranger, took all kinds of pictures from all kinds of angles. Was there no dignity? I was horrified. I couldn't wait to get out of there and never have to look at that battered breast again.

My husband, Pat, wanted me to tell everyone. But I didn't want to tell anyone. I would share when I was ready, and I wasn't ready. I wanted people to see *me*, to know *me*—not just the cancer, not that I had some diagnosis. Maybe a part of me was in denial. Or, more than that, maybe I just didn't believe that this could possibly be true, and that I could choose. I thought to myself:

No way, no how is this going to happen.
No way, no how am I going to have cancer.
No way, no how am I going to be a pity case for people.
HELL NO! THIS IS NOT GOING TO HAPPEN.
I am walking away from this disease.

This is going to be on MY terms.
My life, my terms.

People that knew, mostly close family, wanted to take care of me. My Sicilian mom wanted to come over and cook for me. She wanted to make sure that I was okay and have me rest in bed. I had to tell her one day, "Mom, if you come over and take care of me, I will go to bed and never come out."

So, I kept going. As hard as it was, I kept going. I knew if people started treating me differently—like I had a death sentence—then I was going to die. Dying was not an option. I thought, "No, don't treat me differently; don't take care of me; don't do these things because I need the will to live."

I started receiving cards from kind-hearted people.

"Don't give up."
"We are praying for you."
"I am sorry you are sick."
"Hang in there."

With every card, it was a bigger kick in the gut. *"I am not sick!"* I wanted to yell. "They removed the cancer. Now I am just having preventative treatment. I am *not* sick, and I don't plan on getting sick."

I wondered, "Do they know something that I don't know? Why does everybody think I'm sick?"

Cancer. Not an option. I had already decided. And then I decided that nothing that anybody else said or did would impact my experience. I was not only going to survive, I was going to thrive. What others were feeling or telling me would not be my experience.

I would create my experience and my outcome. It was not easy, but it was simple.

It was a Sunday morning, and Pat and I were going to church. It was the first time I went to church without my wig. I had a short pixie cut. I sat in the pew. I felt exposed. One of my neighbors was walking back to her seat, and she spotted me. She gave me a thumbs up with a big smile. She loved my new bold, rocking haircut. She didn't know what I had just been through. I silently chuckled inside. That admiration of my bold new look gave me a sense of empowerment. And I thought, "Look how far I have come, everything that I have been through." I felt strong, but I also felt a little bit like a fraud.

I am ready now. I am ready to share my story. I am at peace with it. And I got to choose. I got to share my story on my terms. I got through it. I survived and now I am thriving.

I believe that by being bold during my diagnosis—by deciding that the diagnosis was not going to be my reality—I survived. Had I focused on everything that could've gone wrong and all the negatives and played into everyone else's experience, I wouldn't be here today. But I would not accept that.

Nine and half years later, I had my yearly oncology appointment. Dr. Teston looked at me at the end of our visit and said, "You're coming up on 10 years. I don't like to use the word 'cured,' but you don't have to see me anymore." I looked at her blankly. For the first time in nine and half years, I breathed a sigh of relief.

I did it.
I did it.
I really did it.

As she walked out, she smiled and patted my shoulder and said, "You look great, Kathy." I got dressed and walked into the elevator alone. I smiled, and I could feel the tears run down my cheeks. I walked out of the elevator outside, removed my mask and took a deep breath. Then I walked a little taller toward the rest of my beautiful life. I did it! And you can too.

"And I saw that she was powerful and beautiful, not weak and small."

Change Your Story, Change Your Life
Kim Bowers-Antolick

It was 12:45 pm, and the Zoom call was starting in 15 minutes. I had my new notebook, my favorite pen and a tall glass of water sitting next to my laptop on the kitchen table. The laptop was propped up to capture the perfect angle for my face, and the lights were adjusted so I looked my best. Everything in the camera's view was in order: the dishes were put away and the counter was clean; the pile of mail was swept off the island; and the door to the cluttered pantry was closed.

I rushed up the stairs to put on my black shirt, the one with the cap sleeves that makes me look skinny. I checked the mirror. My makeup was in place, and I passed the brush through my hair one last time to get it just right. Ok, I was ready.

I got situated in front of the screen when: "Oh no! I forgot the lip gloss!" I reached for my purse and smoothed the gloss over my lips for the perfect natural glow.

Soon the call was cruising along, and the leader introduced the first exercise: "If you had only a day to live, what message would you share with the world, and what personal story is attached to that message?"

My story! The one that I would share on a global stage; the one that would be published around the world later that year.

Right away, those old familiar feelings bubbled up . . . angst in my belly and tension in my shoulders. I felt warm, and my breath became shallow.

What if I don't come up with the perfect story? I really need to get this right because so many people will be watching. What if my story isn't as good as the others? What will people think of my story?

I was immobilized and stuck. When I glanced at the screen, everybody else seemed to be writing with ease—no problems, no hang ups.

Over the next few days, I continued trying to craft my story. As I rifled through memories, trying to come up with something that would "measure up," I kept seeing my 5-year-old self—a skinny little blonde girl in a pretty green dress—on her first day of kindergarten. All the kids were playing around her—running cars across the carpet, stacking blocks and coloring pictures while she sat at her desk crying because she wanted to be at her Grammy's house, not in some new strange place. Some of the kids were looking at her. She felt so many little eyes. She wondered:

What are they thinking of me? What's wrong with me? Why can't I do it like the other kids?

Memories of this intimidated and unsure little girl continued to haunt me whenever I sat down to write. She kept showing up. She was persistent. It was as if she was trying to tell me something.

A few weeks later, while working on the story and listening to the same old narrative in my mind, it dawned on me! Wait! This *is* my story! This is what I do to myself! I allow all these limiting thoughts to immobilize me and keep me small and unsure like that little girl. Thoughts like:

You might not be good enough. You better look like you have it all together. You have to get it exactly right.

I have often allowed others' perceptions of me to be more important than my own. More important than being who I truly am!

Just as I realized this, I saw her again. But, this time it was different. She wasn't crying. Instead, she looked at me with those big, brilliant blue eyes, and she said:

"It's time to choose a new story! *You* are enough! Everything doesn't need to be perfect. The kitchen can be messy sometimes. You don't have to have every hair in place. Let's tell a new story now!"

And so I listened to her.

Instead of seeing her through others' eyes, I looked through my own. And I saw that she was powerful and beautiful, not weak and small. She was big and brave to allow herself to feel what was true for her in that moment and to express it. I love her.

It never really mattered what anyone else thought about her. I have since changed my story about that little girl, and it's changing my life! Now I'll do Zoom calls right after exercising, and the kitchen isn't perfect when guests come to visit. I have fun writing stories, and I'm free to go to the grocery store without any makeup!

I believe that every moment is an opportunity to tell yourself a new story, and when you change your story, you change your life.

So, here I am. Kim. And this is my story.

"If that had been the end of my life, would I have been proud of who I had become?"

The Gift of Regret
Gregory Mang

About six years ago, I took a guy's trip to Cancun. It was my first time in Mexico, and I was eager to make it a memorable vacation.

One day, I was on the beach with two of my closest friends in the world: Bernard and Caustan.

The sun was radiant, the skies were crystal clear and the breeze was warm. Bernie and I were both in the water while Caustan remained on the beach. The waves began to escalate, and after shrugging one off, I noticed that my feet were barely hitting the sand. I quickly realized that an undertow was starting to pick up.

"Okay, Greg," I told myself, "It's time to get back to the shore." But as I made my way back, I heard Bernie's voice:

"Greg! Help! Help!"

I turned and saw that Bernie had been carried out by the undertow even farther away from the beach than I had. He was waving his arms above the water to get my attention.

The waves crashed harder. When the next one hit Bernie, his head disappeared beneath it.

I immediately made my way to him. He needed me! When I reached him, he bear-hugged me. The next wave *slammed* into us, pulling us both underwater. I couldn't use my arms, so I kicked my legs as hard as I could.

When we surfaced again, my lungs were burning. I could barely breathe.

The waves relentlessly hammered us. One particularly strong wave hit, and I took in a big gulp of salty sea water. I spat it out. I couldn't get enough air into my lungs between the waves. A single thought hijacked my brain:

Oh, God. We might die out here . . .

At that rate, I knew that we wouldn't last much longer.

I look over my shoulder at Bernie: "You gotta get off me, man! Grab my arm! And we'll swim back!"

We grabbed arms and started to make our way back to the safety of the shore, which seemed miles away.

The next wave hit—the strongest one yet. It ripped our grip apart. When I surfaced again, I frantically looked for Bernie. He had been carried even farther away out to sea.

That's when it hit me:

I can't save him. Not like this.
If I try again, chances are I'll get us both killed.
But, at the same time, I can't leave him. He's my brother.

So, I called out to him: "I'm not leaving you, but I need to get help! Keep your head above the water!"

I begrudgingly turned my back to Bernie and faced the beach. By that point, the people almost looked like ants. I waved my arms in the air, hoping to grab someone's attention. In the distance, by some miracle, Caustan saw me and rushed to grab a lifeguard.

The lifeguard leapt down from his tall chair and made his way toward us. I called out to Bernie: "A lifeguard is on the way. I'm not leaving, I'm still here!"

But something was wrong. The lifeguard couldn't make it out to us. The waves had become too strong.

A second lifeguard jumped down from another tower to help the first. I treaded water between the waves, my head on a swivel:

Eyes on Bernie.
Eyes on the lifeguards.
Back and forth.

"I'm still here, man! I'm not going anywhere! Keep your head above the water! The lifeguards are on their way!"

I was tanked. I could only imagine what Bernie was experiencing at that point. I knew that if he didn't resurface between the relentless waves, I'd have to swim back out to try and rescue him again. And I knew that I might not make it. But how could I live with myself if I didn't try?

Dear God, just help Bernie keep his head above the water . . .

An eternity went by.

The lifeguards made their way to me, and it took all three of us to rescue my friend. We finally made it back to shore—Bernie held up by me and one of the lifeguards.

Bernie was exhausted and coughing out water. But all that mattered was that he was alive and safe. As we watched the lifeguards attend to him, Caustan turned to me and said, "For a minute, I thought I was going to lose two brothers out there."

In that moment, it didn't fully sink in just how close Bernie and I had come to the end.

However, in the days, weeks and months that followed, I would periodically get jolted by the memory of that day on the beach and the paralyzing realization that it could have easily gone a different way.

And that realization was typically followed by the question:

If that had been the end of my life, would I have been proud of who I had become?

And the truth?

No.

As a relatively young person in their early 30s, I had up to that point naively believed that I had all the time in the world:

To settle down.
To start my own small business.

To visit Hawaii.
To explore a passion for creative writing.
To tell my family that I loved them.

That day in Cancun, however, was a painful and sobering, yet empowering, reminder that I didn't have all the time in the world, and that I wasn't yet the person who I wanted to be.

While the regret was agonizing, it ultimately led me to a life-defining realization:

The overwhelming regret I was experiencing wasn't being mournful about the past as much as it was being proactive about the future.

I've come to believe that regret is only a burden when we continually choose to ignore it. However, when we choose to experience it in the present moment, regret becomes a guide for all of our actions moving forward.

Regret can remind us of who we truly are and who we desire to become. It can help ensure that we live a life with joy in our hearts and peace in our souls. When we approach regret from this perspective, we transform it from a burden into a blessing.

Regret is a gift. Seize it.

"Choosing me and figuring out what I love and what my gifts are isn't selfish."

Falling in Love with Becoming
Jennifer Jubilado Sbalcio

It was the morning of September 21, 2018 . . . about 4:45 am . . . and I woke up to my husband, Dave, talking on the phone in the other room. It was early, and I could feel in my gut that something was wrong, so I ran over to him. He turned to me and said, "Dad had a stroke and it's not good." I could barely process it. I immediately jumped into action looking for flights and figuring out what else we needed to do.

It was the longest plane ride of my life. When we arrived at the hospital, Dad was on a ventilator, but he was already gone. He was such a wonderful man, and his loss was unexpected and devastating.

In the following months, we lost my dad's best friend, Pat, and my cousin Lorraine, who was only 39 years old. We lost our tax guy, Lenny. We lost both of my cousin Sharon's grandparents, George and Eleanor. We even lost my grandmother, Serafina.

As we put together picture boards for my grandmother's funeral, I remembered how she would make us laugh and giggle all the time, especially when she would say things like, "I have no aching body. I can still run!" Or the way she said, "Oh boy!"

I wondered, "If I died today, what would people remember about me, and how would I feel about the life that I lived?"

Am I the person I wanted to become?
Have I been living the way I was meant to live?
Have I been loving the way I was meant to love?
Have I done what I came here to do?

I knew my answer was "no."

In that moment, I realized that I wanted to *live*, I wanted to *love* and I wanted to *do* so much more—for myself, my family and even the world. I had no clue what that meant or how I was going to get there, but I knew I was going to figure it out. And that was when my journey began.

One day, I came across an invitation from Dean Graziosi and Tony Robbins to become a Knowledge Broker. I didn't even know what that meant, but I signed up anyway. Then I found Maya Comerota's *Born For This* program and thought, "I know there *must* be something I am born to do," so I signed up. Then I joined Christine Michelle's *Create an Aligned Business by Design* class, where I discovered human design and that I wanted to be an entrepreneur.

I discovered that there was something inside of me, and it started to come alive!

I continued investing in myself—in courses, challenges and coaching. I signed up for *Your Uncluttered Home, Made to Do This, High Performance Coaching* and *Masterworks Healing*.

I learned so much about myself.

I learned that I was mindlessly shopping and accumulating to distract myself and numb my feelings. I learned I had a hard time letting go, but once I started clearing the clutter, I was open to receiving so much more. I learned that having a specific person or charity in mind to give my stuff to made it so much easier to let go. In working through this for myself, I learned that I loved helping others mentally and physically clear their clutter so they could love their life and have everything they truly desired too.

I learned that I crave connection and want to be loving, supportive and encouraging as a wife, daughter, sister, cousin, aunt and friend. I learned that I desire to be world-class. And more than just wanting to be world-class, I learned that *I am world-class.*

I learned that there is so much I want to say and do but, up until now, I didn't feel comfortable or confident expressing my feelings. I would suppress them, and then they would erupt like an emotional volcano. I learned that by allowing myself to feel and share, I can actually create connections with myself and others.

I learned that I love being playful and helpful instead of angry and closed off. I learned that I love wearing a flower in my hair. I learned that I love making Dave laugh by coming up with silly names and songs about our dog, Maximus, like "Henry Tinkler" or "Maximoosey, he's got a nice caboosey."

I learned that my life doesn't have to be angry and stressed, but that I can choose and decide to have fun and dream huge freaking dreams. I learned that meditating can be hard, but doing it consistently really calms me and helps me get out of my head.

I learned that choosing me and figuring out what I love and what my gifts are isn't selfish. I learned that I could fall in love with this life I am creating and the person I'm learning about and becoming.

I learned that I have a desire to run my own empire—multiple companies with the help of a world-class, kick-ass team. Who knew? Companies where I can help people breathe life into their lives and experience life and love the same way I do, through giving and receiving. Companies that help spread positivity in the world and help people laugh, smile and matter.

And so, in honor of everyone that I have lost and everyone that I love, I'm going to do just that or die happy and courageously trying.

I believe that we can all choose and decide to live a life we are absolutely in love with. But to do so, we must first fall in love with ourselves and fall in love with becoming.

*"Life is about challenging the status quo
and creating a new dream
full of passion, love and creativity.
It is about releasing limitations
so you are free to live the boldest, bravest
expression of who you are meant to be."*

— *Maya Comerota*

"I was really proud to know that I could rely on me."

Take Flight
Elayne Ireland

Growing up, my father always encouraged us to try new opportunities. He would say, "You rarely regret the things you try, but you often regret the ones you don't." He had his private pilot's license and loved to talk about his flying days. He would tell us about his personal plane and all the incredible times that he enjoyed from the sky.

I loved hearing his stories, imagining the scenery while discovering new places. And I longed to experience those thrills. So, at my father's suggestion, I decided to take flying lessons. My brother Stuart always dreamed about being an airplane mechanic, but his dream ended when he was killed in a motor vehicle accident. I wanted to fly in honor of my father and in remembrance of my brother.

I loved my lessons and my instructor. He was always by my side in the cockpit, so I was never afraid. One day, we were doing "touch and gos" where we'd take off, make four turns in the sky and practice landings, but instead of coming to a stop, we'd take off again. We had repeated four or five of them that particular day before my instructor said we were going in for a complete landing. When I brought the plane to a full stop, he jumped out and said, "Take it up. You're ready for your solo."

I had two choices: to panic or to trust. I could freeze, or I could fly. There I was, excited and pumped up from the previous touch and gos, but shocked that the moment for my solo had arrived. I didn't even have time to think about it! My instructor believed in me; he believed I was ready. Maybe I could. Maybe it was my time. Maybe it was time for me to fly!!

So I did it. Flaps were at zero and the ailerons were into the wind. I smoothly applied full power to increase RPMs. I maintained runway alignment, applied the right rudder and, as the plane accelerated, I pulled the elevator back to lift the nose wheel off the ground. I kept the top of the cowling on the horizon and the wings level as I reached my climbing speed before leveling off.

I was doing it!
I was flying!
I was flying an airplane all by myself!!

I made my first turn, made my second turn, made my third turn and my fourth. But on the descent, fear started to take hold. I saw graphic images of my brother's accident: his crunched up car, the mangled eucalyptus tree, blood stains and used medical supplies scattered at the scene.

I thought, "No way would God take two of my parents' children; no way will both of us be taken." I concentrated on what I needed to do for a safe landing. I throttled back, allowed the cowling to lower and adjusted pitch for descent. I prayed to my brother, "Stu, please let me see Pooh and Pops again; please carry me down safely. Come on, Stu, give me the strength to land this plane." My legs were shaking, my eyes were filled with tears. Yet somehow, I touched down, and I earned my wings.

I was so proud knowing how happy my dad was going to be. But more than that, I was really proud to know that I could rely on *me*. Being the youngest of four, I rarely got the opportunity to be the first at anything.

Since then, I've taken many more first flights: I moved to California by myself; I left an abusive marriage; and I became a strong advocate for my daughter Rebecca, who faces the challenges of Down syndrome.

I believe moving forward is the path through fear and limitation, and that we're all born with wings.

"I knew that I was not going to be the woman whose dreams died in her diary."

Dreams Are for Living
Georgeta Geambasu

When I was a little girl in Romania, I wanted to play piano so badly. I would constantly ask my mum: "*Mama, mama pot te rog sa iau lectii de pian?*" "Mum, could I take piano classes, please please, please???"

And my mum would say swiftly, "Oh sweetheart, we cannot afford it."

Also when I was a little girl and people asked, "What do you want to be when you grow up," I would respond, "I want to be a writer!!!" And I believed it! But my mum would say, "She likes stories, but this will change. She will be an engineer."

Forty years later, on a Sunday morning, March 15, I sat in my house with my two kids and husband. I had a great family and a great job. I kept busy every day with all the things that needed to be done for family and for work. I said "yes" to everything and made sure that everyone's needs were met. I moved to the beautiful land of Switzerland. My life was like a picture perfect postcard. It *seemed* great. But there was a part of me that longed for something. There was a whisper and a rumble inside me for more. I just wasn't certain what the whisper was saying, *yet.*

That morning, I was listening to the happy gigglings of my 11-year-old twins, Léa and Horia. Sorin, my husband, was playing with them, and my heart swelled. I went to join them when the phone rang. It was my brother. "Hello Geo, I don't know how to say what I have to say. Please sit. Mum passed away this morning. Because we are in quarantine, I don't think you can come. I am so sorry."

It felt like the air froze around me. I broke into tears and fell to my knees, crying. I heard words, but I didn't understand them. Though my family embraced me, I felt alone and empty.

I walked to my bedroom robotically. I lowered the blinds to be alone in the dark. I moved around the room in search of something. Something was leading me. I found it. It was a picture of my mum and a diary.

I lit a candle, placed the picture aside and began to read. My mum was such a talented writer. I vividly re-lived her stories; I sensed her humour; I saw her laughing with her best friend; I saw her pensive mood as she wrote her words. I felt warmth and light inside.

But as I read deeper into the diary, I came upon other fragments of her story—her dreams that went unlived.

Daca as fi avut curaj as facut scoala de soferi . . . daca nu imi era frica sa calatoresc singura m-as fi intalnit cu Geo in Paris . . .

Dreams to drive a car one day . . . dreams to go to Paris . . .

My mum had regrets for not having said what she wanted to say . . . for not doing what she wanted to do . . . for forgetting to live . . .

"Oh Mum," I thought, "I didn't know you felt this way." My body felt cold and full of sorrow. I start to think of my own life.

Am I really living?
If my life is so great, why am I anxious about my future?
Why am I so busy, busy, busy?
What happened to my dreams?
Where did that little whisper go—the whisper of the dreams, of the piano,
of all the things I loved?

I took a deep breath, surrendered and recognized that I was getting caught in all the *doing*. *Doing* my job. *Doing* all the things that needed to be done for the family. I realized I had stopped dreaming. Instead, I had focused on all the *doing*, and I'd stopped really *living*.

I leaned into the despair that I was feeling. I searched for the meaning.

Everything happens for a reason. Perhaps this is a gift. A last gift from my mum.

I didn't know what to do, but I knew that I was not going to be the woman whose dreams died in her diary. I made a decision.

I would *live* my dreams. I would do the things that I *love* to do!

That was a year and a half ago. Oh Mum, if you could only see me now going after my dreams!

Today, I have a beautiful new black piano in the house. I play every day. I am writing a book—a memoir, *From the Head to the Heart*, to share how I started dreaming again and connecting to my feelings. I want my children to know how to do it too. I am writing just like I dreamed! Sometimes . . . I even dare to say "NO!" *gasp*

Thank you, Mum . . . you made me realize that dreams are meant to be lived. They are not meant to die in a diary.

"My voice is the source of my strength and power."

No More Secrets
Michelle Lachner

I was 19 years old and full of hope—the last of four siblings to join the military, and it was finally my turn. I was so proud of myself, not just because I was serving my country, but I was a woman serving my country! I wore my Air Force blues while waiting to board a plane for Spain where I was being stationed. I thought:

I can leave everything behind.
I don't have to think of the past.
Everything will be new—a new country, a new home, a new job.
There will be new people.
I can totally reinvent myself, and no one has to know.
I can't wait for this fresh start!

It was two weeks into my new life in Madrid, Spain. Late one night, I was walking home to my barracks. It was dark outside, and all I could see was their glistening lights 100 yards away. All of a sudden I felt danger. I heard footsteps from behind, and I started to run. As I was being chased, I thought, "This can't be happening again!" This time, I screamed at the top of my lungs: "Help! Help! Help!" He tackled me to the ground. A guy from the barracks heard me. He raced over and charged my attacker, yelling, "Run Michelle! Run!" As I ran, I thought:

Why?
What did I do to deserve this?
Did I say something?
Did I look at them a certain way?
Am I putting out some kind of vibe?

When I was raped at 16, I kept it a secret. I was afraid of what people would think.

Would they believe me . . . still love me . . . accept me?
Would they think it's my fault?
Would they think I deserved it?

I just wanted to forget it. I wanted it to go away. I felt so alone and ashamed, and somehow I felt that I was to blame.

For the next 40 years, I had constant nightmares. I would wake up screaming in the middle of the night. I never felt safe. I was anxious and depressed. I suffered panic attacks. I had anorexia. It got to a point, after another horrible nightmare, where I couldn't keep it in any longer.

I walked into my regular 8:00 am Monday appointment with Dr. Washinsky, and I chose to tell him what had been going on for the last 40 years and share the secrets that had been haunting me. I told him of the constant nightmares, the anxiety and depression. He looked at me and said, "Michelle, you have PTSD (post-traumatic stress disorder)." I said, "Oh no, I wasn't even in combat. I can't have PTSD."

"No, you do have PTSD, Michelle. It's from the sexual assaults." He gave me the name of Dr. Tart, a specialist in sexual trauma. I went home and googled "sexual assault and PTSD," and there it was . . . page after page after page. "The number one cause of women to have PTSD . . . sexual assault." Story after story, headline after headline. How could I not know? This thing had taken my life for 40 years, and I didn't even know! Not any more! They may have taken my body back then, but they couldn't have me now!

Now I get to decide!
Now I get to choose!
Now I get to speak.
They don't get to take more life from me than they already have.
This stops now!
This is my life, my voice and I'm taking control.

I picked up the phone and made an appointment with Dr. Tart.

It's been three years since that initial phone call with Dr. Tart. During that time, I've been on a healing journey of finding my voice, sharing my story and helping others do the same. I'm no longer afraid of what people will think. I'm not afraid of what people will say. I'm not afraid of being me. I am in control of my life. My voice is the source of my strength and power.

I write this knowing that in a few minutes I will be sharing my story on national news. I look in the mirror and see my reflection and think, "I'm so proud of the woman I've become. I'm strong, confident and unafraid."

I share my story to save others from experiencing the same thing, and, more than that, I share my story to save myself. I believe that some secrets are not meant to be kept. If and when you have the courage to share, those same secrets will support you to shine.

"With this revelation, I was able to shift my thoughts. I became happier, more playful, more creative."

Transformation Through Tenderness
Atiya Chaudhry-Green

It was one winter's gloomy afternoon, and I was at Victoria Junior school in a little town called Burton-on-Trent. It was the early 1970s, and I was 7 years old. The headmistress informed the teachers to usher the children into the great assembly hall.

We sat on the floor in our class rows. We were excited, and the hall was full of chatter. Then Mrs. Blackberry and Mr. Wildsmith manoeuvred in a big trolley with a TV perched on top of it. Mrs. Blackberry shouted, "Quiet everyone!" The TV switch clicked, and the "Sooty and Sweep" show came on. It was a show with two puppet characters that went on adventures and bickered with each other.

The assembly hall was very quiet; only the echoes of the TV characters' voices could be heard. We were watching the show intently . . . when all of a sudden, I shrieked, "He's over there!"

At that moment, a thousand eyeballs of children and teachers turned to look at me. The programme continued, and everyone went back to watching *except me*! I sat there repeating terrible thoughts for its duration:

You are so stupid!
It's not real; it's a TV programme!
You just made yourself look stupid!

That night, I didn't sleep well as the scene played again and again in my head. Over the next few days the memory faded . . . but so did my joy and happiness. It was the start of many years during which I stopped speaking up in groups and sharing my thoughts.

Twenty-five years later, my older brother Teak visited the family. Usually during his visits he looked exhausted—his eyes sunken and grey. But that visit was different. He looked more alive—10 years younger, sparkly and bright. He even asked us how we were, which he'd never done before!

I was curious about what could have caused such a dramatic change. He said, "I am taking an NLP (neuro-linguistic programming) course."

I wondered: "If this helped Teak so much . . . what is possible for me? Could this help me become more alive? Happier?"

I signed up for the NLP course immediately.

At one session, the trainer invited us to think about something in our lives that had been holding us back. I wanted to understand why I didn't speak up in groups. It seemed like a recurring pattern in my life. As I explored, I realized that the first memory of this was the scene of me at age 7 in the assembly hall.

Oh my! I finally understood what happened! That memory got trapped in my subconscious without me even being aware of it. I then replayed those circumstances in my mind day after day and year after year. And my ego would try to protect me by saying:

Don't speak in groups . . . you know what happened last time.
You don't want everyone to look at you . . . to laugh at you.
Just stay quiet, and it will be ok.

These thoughts played out in my adulthood and affected my ability to express my essence and be happy and joyful the way children (and adults) should be. And I hadn't even been aware it was happening!

With this revelation, I was able to shift my thoughts. I became happier, more playful, more creative. I had more fun and laughed more. I started to share in groups more often and with less effort.

It got me thinking . . .

What if children were supported to reflect, reframe and realign negative experiences to become resilient instead of having the negative experience completely frame who they become as adults?

What if my teacher had been tender with me to explore my feelings after my outburst and reframed the situation by focusing on the unique, extraordinary gift of my imagination—that I was able to put myself in the TV programme's scene?

What if my parents asked me how my day at school was and listened with compassion and curiosity to support me to rewrite the experience so it didn't affect my ability to talk in groups into adulthood?

Now I have the honor and privilege of being able to bring this work to the world. I support children (and adults) to be fully alive and free to be who they are created to be by reframing negative experiences to release trauma and cultivate freedom.

"Any other time I would've given myself permission to give up. Not that day."

Just Listen
Jennifer Wallace Alvarez

It was February 2017.

I had been popping ibuprofen since December to control the constant headaches that came with celiac disease if even the tiniest bit of gluten accidentally came my way. The headaches turned to migraines if I ignored them. For all the other symptoms—brain fog, joint pain, insomnia, GI problems—I simply pushed through. I was busy with my little girl, Bella—the light of my life—my work and volunteering. I thought, "I don't have time to feel sick. I've wasted far too much time already. I'm not losing any more."

So, I dealt with it the best way I knew how. Even though the voice in my head kept telling me:

You are sick.
There is something wrong.
Go to the ER.

Weeks passed. I got more and more tired. I heard the voice again in my head:

Go to the ER.

"No," I thought, "I have too much work to do, too many commitments. I don't have time to go to the ER. I'll be fine."

I wasn't *fine.*

One morning, while I was on a photo shoot for a preschool, my chest tightened and I couldn't breathe. It felt as though my chest had been kicked by a horse. I keeled over.

I heard Diane, the preschool director and my friend, yell, "Call 911!"

I thought, "No! What about the kids? What about my work?"

I heard the voice in my head say:

GO TO THE ER!

I didn't want to go to the ER. I just wanted to go home and see *my* baby. But I knew I *must* listen to the voice that time.

At the hospital, the doctors surrounded me. One of them said, "You had a small heart attack and you overdosed on ibuprofen."

I screamed in my head, "How can this be happening?! I'm only 40 years old!! If you had listened to yourself, you wouldn't be in this situation."

That voice knew all along. I just didn't listen. And I didn't act. It had been telling me for years. The voice would talk to me, and I would ignore it.

Not. Any. More.

Something had to change. From then on, I would listen. From then on, I would act. I promised myself. I knew I had to. My life literally depended on it.

A month later, I scrolled through Facebook where I saw an ad for a 30-day clean-eating challenge. As I started to scroll past it, the voice said:

Just do it.

So I listened.

The voice continued to tell me to do things and go places. It told me to join programs and communities to discover my purpose and passion. I didn't always understand it, but I always listened. And as I did, the voice got louder and louder. My symptoms started to go away; I didn't need those huge bottles of ibuprofen. I became healthier. I became happier. My inner voice became a loud and constant friend.

I was invited to an incredible retreat with other women for connection, transformation and surfing! Up until then, I was always afraid to surf, and that fear kept my toes in the sand.

But the voice said:

Heck yes!

You have always wanted to surf.
This is your time.
Just do it!

So I leaned into that fear, and I packed my bags for Costa Rica.

As soon as I arrived, I put on my bathing suit and jumped in the water with my surfboard. Before I even reached the lineup, two waves came stacked together; I was not ready for the second one. It caught the nose of my board, and I dove under it. Then the board and the force of the water all came crashing down on my head.

Any other time I would've given myself permission to give up. Not that day. I just quieted myself and listened. The voice came:

Take your time.

So I did. I stayed out there. I watched the incoming waves and collected myself. I said, "When I am ready, baby steps will be fine." I heard the voice:

You CAN do this.

And then I realized, I *am* doing this and this is *so fun*! *I am surfing*!

As I stood on that surfboard riding the wave, I said "thank you" out loud.

"Thank you" to me.
"Thank you" to my body.
"Thank you" to the voice.

For the first time, I felt completely alive and free.

Listening to that voice saved my life. And even more than that . . . it helped me fall in love with it!

I know it can do the same for yours.

"I had to bring back his will to live. I knew what to do."

Rise Up
Judit Hora

It was a beautiful autumn weekend with golden leaves and fresh crisp mountain air in October 2015. I was riding in our car with my husband, Elliot, and four of our five children: Josefina, Gábor, Sonia and Denise. Francis, our oldest, was unable to join us as he had some work obligations. The six of us pulled up to the driveway of the small ski village resort, Ribnica Pohorje, in Slovenia to meet our friends for a retreat. The place was buzzing with life. The men stood in a circle passionately sharing their latest adventures, and the children ran around exploring the property.

The next day, the whole group hiked up to the summit of the mountain to a gorgeous lake among the rolling hills. I held Elliot's hand and took in the breathtaking view surrounding us.

"We should head back," Elliot said. And we began driving down a steep narrow mountain road with no railing on the sides. Suddenly, our car hit a cement boulder.

I got out of the car to check the damage. When I turned back to tell Elliot what I saw, he was slouched over the steering wheel, unconscious. I ran over to his side and realized that I needed to pull his body out. I thought:

How will I ever be able to pull him out?
Will I be strong enough?
He has to make it!

I managed to get him out halfway when I heard him make three death-rattling sounds. I'd never heard such sounds in my life, and I wondered what was happening. I laid him down in the middle of this one-lane dirt road. I looked at his chest; it was not rising. He was not breathing. Costi, our Romanian friend who was with us, checked his pulse. There was none.

Our three daughters were crying and praying over him. Josefina, my oldest, screamed out, "No, I won't let you take away my daddy!" My whole body shivered, and it felt as though the air was frozen around us. My mind raced; I thought of the stories and the miracles in the Bible—how Jesus made Lazarus rise up from the dead by commanding him, "Come forth!" And Lazarus did. And how, when Jesus spoke with the little girl, he said, "Little girl, arise!"

Follow his example, Judit.
Just follow his example.

I looked at Elliot. "Rise up, get up, honey," I said while praying to God for a miracle.

Please God. Please let him live. Please God. I will do whatever it takes, just please let him live.

I got down next to him on the ground. I gave him CPR and did the chest compressions:

One.

Two.

Three.

Four . . . I could barely remember how it was done.

The others were all standing around us in a circle. I leaned over Elliot and breathed into his mouth. As I got ready for the second set of chest compressions, I suddenly heard his voice from above. I looked up to my right and saw that he was standing beside me. He was looking down at me, asking, "What are you looking for on the ground?" and he also started to look around. I thought to myself:

How is this possible?!
I was just leaning over him!
How can he be standing beside me!?

After the ambulance arrived, it took us to the hospital in Slovenj Gradec. We found out Elliot had suffered an abdominal aneurysm. My cousin, Kristina, who is a doctor, told me that more than 90 percent of those with abdominal aneurysms die within five minutes; when the ambulance arrives at the hospital, they are usually dead.

No, he can't die. He will live!!!

Hours passed, and Elliot was rushed to the operating room. His blood vessel burst again; another 1.5 quarts of blood flowed into his abdomen area. This was too much. I sent our kids and totaled car on a trailer back to Hungary while he underwent a second operation. I was not certain how long it would be. The operation was successful, but Elliot needed to stay in the ICU for a whole week. I sat at his bedside all day, grateful that he was alive. I only left his side in the evening to go to bed. When I got back in the morning, he was worse than when I left him. He continued to get worse each day. He was connected to tubes and machines.

No. This can't happen. You must survive! There is so much to live for! I love you. Your children love you. It is not your time.

I had to bring back his will to live. I knew what to do. I started to sing—gospel songs, songs of praise, marching songs, all the songs we would listen to together.

"Standing on the promises of Christ my King, through eternal ages let His praises ring . . ."

"Oh, Lord my God when I am in awesome wonder, consider all the world Thy hands have made . . ."

"Keep on believing God answers prayer, Keep on believing He's still up there . . ."

I saw a vision: I was cooking at the stove in our kitchen, looking out to our dining area; it felt like no one was at home and I was totally alone.

I thought to myself, "I am *not* going home alone." My body shivered. I knew I was not going home alone.

"Elliot is walking out the hospital door with me!" I declared.

I kept singing.
I kept praying.
I kept believing.
I kept breathing life into his life.

Whenever the nurses and doctors asked me to leave and go home, I did not dare go. I knew what I must do.

I kept singing.

I kept praying.
I kept believing.
I kept breathing life into his life.

Day by day, week by week, he started getting better. The nurses and doctors came. Everyone was baffled. They brought others to come and see the miracle that was happening.

Three weeks later, we were finally at home, reunited with our children. At 5:00 am, Elliot got up. He looked at me with his sweet eyes and said, "I know it is early . . . would it be possible for you to make me something to eat? I am really hungry."

"Of course, of course!" I got up from bed and made my way to the kitchen, so grateful he was home. So grateful he was alive.

As I stood by the stove and cooked eggs for him, I looked out into the dining area where he was sitting at the table. Tears flowed like a river down my face. I realized that *this* was the exact moment I saw in my vision.

But he was there.
He was alive.
I was not alone.
It was a miracle.

Hallelujah!

I believe that it is possible to breathe life into another's life. If you have *faith* and *believe* it is possible, miracles *will* happen.

"All those years I had learned to quiet my own feelings and quiet my voice under the guise of 'being fine.'"

When Feelings Are Fine
Jenny Infante-Reyes

Disneyland! I was 6 years old, and it was my very first trip on an airplane. We were going to meet Mickey, Donald and Pluto in real life! I was so excited, but I also knew I had to show my mom I was grown up enough for the trip. So, I carried my backpack by myself and buckled myself in my seat. I thought, "I can even go to the bathroom by myself." I stood up to go, but my mom stopped me and said, "'No just wait—I'll take you later."

"No mom. It's fine. I can do it," I said, standing tall with my shoulders back and my head held high.

I felt like such a big girl as I pulled the latch closed, I did my thing (I washed my hands) and then—oh no! The latch wouldn't move. It was stuck. *gasp*

I panicked.

Am I stuck here forever?

Does anyone know that I'm in here?
Was my mom right: I can't trust myself?

Eventually the flight attendant opened the door; my mom was standing outside. I ran straight for her, tears welling up, but she caught my eye and said, "Shhh… we don't do that here."

We walked back to our seats, and I started to speak, but she dismissed it and said, "It's ok, you're fine." And that was that.

Twelve years later, I was 18 and in a family meeting over my grandfather's estate. I was a beneficiary, and it was my first time to be involved in something so . . . grown up. I wasn't following a discussion, so I began to ask a question. And again I was told, "No need. It's fine."

Fast forward. I was in a new country, married with two kids and running my brand and marketing consultancy. My youngest, Jamie, was 9 and was in gymnastics. I was so proud of her; she was incredible. Her coaches said she was a role model to her teammates.

While driving her to the gym, sometimes she'd say her stomach hurt, or her head hurt or something was wrong with her foot. But I'd brush it off and say, "Drink some water honey, you're ok. It's fine."

One day, she froze and cried. She refused to walk in and said, "Mom, I want to quit."

Shocked, I took her aside. Between tears, Jamie said, "Mom, you're not listening to how I feel. I'm only going because it's making you happy."

That broke my heart. As a mother I knew the one thing I didn't want was for my kids to do only the things that made me happy. I wanted them to have a voice, to feel seen and, most especially, to be heard.

It was painful to realize that she was right—I wasn't listening. I hadn't been listening to her . . . or to myself. All those years I had learned to quiet my own feelings and quiet my voice under the guise of "being fine." But, it wasn't fine anymore.

Today, Jamie is back in gymnastics, and she loves it. We've gotten to a place where we talk about our feelings; how it's ok that sometimes it's not ok. We feel at our own pace. None of it is good or bad, or right or wrong or out of place—it just is. I say *we* because I now practice it too in everything I do with my kids, my clients and even by myself.

I believe our feelings are our voice, and no matter who you are—an entrepreneur, a mother, a wife, a daughter—your voice is meant to be heard.

"At the age of 14, I played 'Revolutionary Etude' despite only having four and a half fingers on my left hand!"

Return to Joy
Michele Vayn

When I was 4 years old, there were no limits to what I would do. I was full of excitement, joy and wonder! I climbed up trees like a squirrel and reached for apples and cherries from the highest branches. I chased butterflies while holding all sorts of different flowers—buddleias, daisies, roses and peonies—to see what flowers they would love the best. I decorated sand castles with sea weeds and feathers. I danced, played piano and made people laugh just by being me. Back then, nobody seemed to mind that I lived by my own rules.

When I turned 7, everything changed.

I visited my grandmother, who used a card wool machine to make mattresses. I was intrigued and wanted to help. When she wasn't paying attention, I walked over to the machine and started to put the wool through. My tiny little fingers were so small that they made it underneath the blade, and a big portion of my left index finger was cut off.

They rushed me to the hospital, but the doctors were unable to save that part of the finger. I was left with half an index finger. After that, my mother, my father and my two sisters, Helene and Dominique, were always worried about me—convinced that I would get myself into trouble or get hurt.

If I wanted to sing, I was told it was too loud. If I wanted to read books, I was too young. If I wanted to stay with a friend, I might get hurt. I was barely allowed to do or say anything. They would say:

Ne cours pas.
Ne saute pas.
Ne fais pas ceci.
Ne fais pas cela.
Tu pourrais te blesser.
La vie est dangereuse.

Don't run.
Don't jump.
Don't move.
Don't disturb anyone.
Don't be too loud.
Don't be silly.
Don't do anything dangerous.

No matter what I wanted to do, the answer was always "NO!" And I soon learned an entirely new way to be.

After about three months, which felt like an eternity, I was a shadow of the little girl I once was. I wanted to disappear. I felt like a nuisance to everyone.

And then there started to be a rumble inside me of discontent and desire . . .

I didn't want to do what they expected of me.
I didn't want to behave.
I didn't want to do everything the safe way.
I wanted to be *me*!!!
I wanted to live *my life*!

The rumbles continued, and they wouldn't go away!

There must be a solution!
There has to be more to life than sitting still, being quiet and playing by
all these crazy rules!
I must be able to DO something!
What can I do?

I decided to do something! I asked myself, "What can I do that no one can stop me from doing?" In an instant I had the answer.

The piano! I can play the piano!

I immediately, like a well behaved girl, asked my parents and Madame Zacchéo: "May I please play the piano again?" Everyone agreed even though I was only 7, and I only had nine and a half fingers.

I made my declaration: "I will, one day, play Chopin's 'Revolutionary Etude.'"

Many people laughed at my fantasy as "Revolutionary Etude" is a very difficult left-hand study. My parents, sisters and friends said, "You will quit in weeks!"

But I had a dream! No matter what my family said, I focused all my energy on making my dream come true.

I would play "Revolutionary Etude" by Chopin!

"Winners never quit!" I thought. I practiced and got lost in the music day after day and month after month.

Seven years of determination later, at the age of 14, I played "Revolutionary Etude" despite only having four and a half fingers on my left hand! As I played, I felt the rush of being exactly who I was born to be and loving life!

Years later, as a young professional, I got lost again in all the rules that seemed to be part of having a successful professional career.

Think as we want you to think.
Do as we want you to do.
Don't question anything.
Don't shine too bright.

I heard the rumble inside me again:

If you are not happy, remember you are in charge.

I enlisted my childlike wonder, determination and curiosity just as I did many years prior. I thought, "I must be able to do something!" An idea came. This time it wasn't to play music about a revolution . . . it was to be one! It was time to bring *joy* back to CEOs and organizations!

I would transform organizations from the inside out! I would change the way things are done so they could be done better and with more joy! And that is what I did. I left my career to find my joy again and to use my gifts and talents to bring it back to leaders and organizations. Now I have the privilege of consulting with CEOs of large and small organizations to support them to bring joy back to their lives and to their workplaces.

I believe that life's purpose is joy, and it takes bold decisions and daring determination to be the person that you are uniquely here to be. Others won't necessarily understand it, but it may just be the permission they need to return to joy too.

"I focused more on that little glow within me."

A Glow in the Dark
Laurette Smith

I used to hate the dark.

In November 2019, I visited my homeland, New Zealand, with my son Grayson. I was so excited to show him my country! I booked a private boat tour into the glow worm caves.

On the day of the tour, we pulled up at a farm—no boat. The guide ushered me into a room, pointed at a pile of clothes and told me, "Take your clothes off, put these on and grab that headgear." I thought, "What? Oh no! I've accidentally booked a *caving* tour, not a boat tour. I hate caves!"

I was terrified, but Grayson was so excited. I couldn't back out. Geared up, we started descending steps—down, down, down until we were 90 feet below the earth—into an *actual* cave.

Dark. Confined. I was shaking. In we went.

It was intense. The passages were so tight! We were climbing up sharp rocks and sliding down the other side. After an *hour* of heart-racing caving, we reached the final passage. I was last in line. I looked behind me and saw this vast darkness of nothing—90 feet of earth above me.

I squeezed through the tiny opening and emerged into an underground cavern. We turned our headlights off and sat in utter darkness. I couldn't even see my hand in front of my face. It was terrifying. I had been running from darkness for most of my life.

I was a super happy kid. I spent my days dancing around in a tutu! Until the day that it all changed.

I was just 7 years old. I walked into my grandfather's room. I always wanted to make him happy because he was such a grouchy old man. That was the day he started raping me. Years of fear and torment followed. I would hide from him in dark, small spaces.

Under the bed.
In closets.
In the tiny compartment above my closet.
In the boot of my mother's car.

I hated the dark.

I grew up, got married and had kids, but spent my days running in fear from that darkness within.

I was in darkness again. No escape. I couldn't run. We waited in silence. My heart raced.

A wee light appeared—a glow worm! I had forgotten where I was! One by one, they started to shine; it looked like a majestic universe.

Beautiful light waiting in the darkness.

I sat in total awe. In that moment, I allowed myself to step into the darkness inside me . . . I sat and waited. I saw it, and I felt it. This teeny glow.

After leaving the cave and the farm, I knew something had shifted inside me. Even Grayson could tell that something had profoundly changed in me. My body shook for a good five hours!

As the weeks went on, I focused more on that little glow within me. It became brighter and brighter. I finally saw me, and I began to heal from the inside out. I came back to life—I even got back into a tutu!

I spent the next year rediscovering who I was, getting trained and licensed in neuro-linguistics and now I help other women find their light and heal.

I believe your light is stronger than any darkness in your life. As you lean into your darkness, your light will find you. Your light is waiting for you . . . to heal you . . . to set you free.

"I didn't quit! I made a choice!"

Choose Happy
Michelle Golz

I was a nurse for 27 years. I loved helping people in their time of need, being at their bedside, visiting with them and making them more comfortable while they were in the hospital. Often, my patients would say, "I just love your smile."

As I walked into the hospital one hot August day, I was curious about my caseload. We were in the midst of the pandemic; I was hoping for a light caseload so I could visit with the patients a bit. It got lonely in the hospital without any visitors, and I relished taking a moment to show the patients that I cared and that they were loved. Since I worked in the ICU, I doubted that my caseload would be light, but I crossed my fingers anyway and hoped for a couple extra moments for visits.

After our RN huddle to start the day, my boss stopped me: "I need you in my office at 2:00 pm."

"What?" I wondered, "Right in the middle of my day?"

"This is strange," I thought. Knowing how she had been treating all the other nurses, I knew it couldn't be good. We had close to 20 people leave that year because she was so hard on everyone.

I walked into her office and was surprised to also see Dawn, my team leader. "What's this all about?" I wondered.

My boss slapped a long, yellow legal pad onto the desk; there was a lot of writing on it.

"Let's start," she said curtly. "You don't know how to hang blood; you don't know chest tubes; you don't know EPIC, charting or art lines."

The tiny room felt like it was closing in on me. I couldn't breathe; I needed air. I was hot.

She continued, "All of the doctors do not think you know what you are doing, and your coworkers do not think you are confident."

I tried to command myself to not cry, but the tears came anyway. I didn't know what to say, so I said nothing. As I walked back to my ICU, I got mad at myself. I thought, "Why didn't you speak up or talk back? You know none of that is true. Why couldn't you be strong and say something?"

As I drove home that night through a lot of traffic, I thought all sorts of crazy thoughts.

How could this happen?
Twenty-seven years of giving and serving.
How could she say those things?
Could that even be true?
I wonder what would happen if I didn't show up to work again?
I wonder what would happen if I just ended things tonight.

Would work even miss me?

As I crawled into bed, my husband, Dave, rolled over and asked, "How was work?"

"I'm tired," I said, and I kissed him goodnight and tried to sleep.

In the morning, as I drank my coffee, Dave called to me: "Honey, can you come upstairs for a minute? I want to introduce you to Bob. He is the financial advisor, and we are going to discuss retirement and review our portfolios."

"Hello Michelle, do you have any questions?" Bob asked.

Suddenly, I had an idea. I did have a question.

"Hmmmm. Yes. Do I have enough money in my 401k to say 'FU' to my employer and walk away?"

It got so silent that you could hear a pin drop. I looked over at Dave. He looked mortified. Bob was chuckling, and I could feel my face turning red. I didn't *ever* use the term "FU!"

After a long minute, Bob responded, "Yes, I think you could walk away."

I could not wait until Monday. That very day, I turned in my notice. I logged on to the Workday app and clicked the button to resign. It took less than 10 minutes. And it was done.

At first I felt happy, excited and free, but after a few weeks, I started to feel sadness and guilt.

Did I do the right thing?

What was I going to do now?

I filled my time in my art room doing anything and everything to forget. And when I wasn't making inspiration art to try to get myself out of my funk, I was scrolling Facebook, Instagram and email.

Then I saw it. An email entitled: "BE THE PERSON YOU WERE BORN TO BE . . . FREE."

Something ignited in me. I was curious. And I thought, "You have nothing better to do, Michelle, so why not? Plus . . . it's free!"

I signed up. I poured my heart in. I poured my soul in. I showed up to the Zoom room early. I did everything the coach, Maya, asked us to do. I played full out like Jerry Rice! I was the first one on the field, aka Zoom, and the last one off. I played hard for *me*! Not anyone else. I felt amazing. Through the process, I began to uncover my message and my story. I started to realize that there was something that I was here to be and do. My life wasn't over; it was just beginning.

But as I wrote my story, I felt sad again. I contacted Maya to ask if I needed a new story. A few moments later, my phone rang. It was Maya. She was calling me!

"What's your story?" she asked.

"I quit my ICU job during the pandemic; I left my friends; I left people that needed help. There isn't enough help there. I feel like I should be happy, but I am not. I quit. I failed."

Then Maya said, "You didn't quit, Michelle, you made a choice."

Immediately, I felt a *huge* weight lift off of me. It was the feeling of truth. I felt at peace.

I didn't quit! I made a choice! I chose to leave a job that wasn't treating me well. A job that so many others wanted to leave but didn't feel they could! I realized right then that *I am that girl*! The one that was strong. The one that would stand up for herself! The one that would stand up for what was right.

Not long after, I was shopping, and I saw a sign that said, "TO BE HAPPY GIVE HAPPY," and it inspired a movement. The Happy Mail movement.

All that art I had been making? It became Happy Mail traveling around the globe to places like Europe, Australia, Canada, the United States and on and on, inspiring smiles and happiness all over the world. Each time I make it, send it or know it arrives, I feel happier, and I get beautiful messages from all over the world about how my Happy Mail makes each person's day a little bit brighter!

My name is Michelle Golz, and I am a HappyPreneur.

"I decided to start living my life as an experiment."

The Infinite Present
Jennifer Poole

When I was 3 years old and my brother James was 4, my family went on a vacation and stopped at a tourist attraction in northern Michigan called Castle Rock. On the side of the road, there was a huge statue of Paul Bunyan and his ox, Babe the Blue Ox, standing at the base of a lookout that overlooked Lake Huron. As we climbed to the top, I struggled to keep up with the family, so my mom picked me up and carried me.

At the top of the lookout, my mom turned to my brother and asked, "James what do you see?" He said, "I see clouds! I see trees! I see water!"

She turned to me and asked, "Jenny, what do you see?" I pointed to the distance and said, "I see God."

Everyone at the top of Castle Rock turned to look at me with my arm outstretched toward the horizon, then turned back to try to see what I was pointing at.

My mom sometimes asked me, "What did you see up there, Jen?" The memory had some lost clarity. And to not risk sounding crazy, I answered something like, "Everything was just so beautiful that I'm sure I related it to heaven on earth."

The truth was that I saw God at the top of that roadside tourist attraction.

Not too long after that day at Castle Rock, I began Sunday school where I saw a picture of God. He was a man with a beard and a white robe surrounded by children who had sheep at his feet. He looked different than I remembered.

Our family took another road trip when I was 6 years old. We drove out west in an orange Ford Torino with no air conditioning. My brother and I played the alphabet game searching for all the letters of the alphabet on the signs that whizzed by. "M!", "N!", "O!", "P!" There were long pauses as we searched for a Q, and then an eternity looking for the last letter. Finally, a Pizza Hut was on the horizon. "Z!" we shouted, and we started the game all over again.

Somewhere along the way, we stopped at another tourist-type attraction. I later found out it was a religious visitor's center.

My eyes got wide as I walked into a round, blue room with arched ceilings and beautiful paintings of clouds and stars and planets on the wall. A huge statue of Jesus with outstretched arms stood in front of me. He seemed to be inviting me and the rest of us hungry road-trippers to seek shelter under his massive arms.

I looked up and saw a quote on the wall. I was just learning to read, and there was a word I didn't recognize. I pointed at the word and asked my mom what it said. "It says 'infinity,'" she explained. "That means forever and ever. No beginning and no end. When we die, we will go to heaven and live forever and ever."

What?!

How can that be? Forever seemed like *such* a long time to exist! That's an awful lot of alphabet games in a hot car!! I thought about that word and what it meant for the rest of the day.

Later that night, we stopped at a Days Inn. Our last name was "Day," so I imagined all Days Inns were built just for us! I jumped into the pool, and after another long, hot day in the car, it felt like heaven to float in the cool water. I was sure that I could stay there forever. "Maybe infinity isn't such a bad thing after all," I thought.

After the trip, my mind kept going back to that word and what it meant. One night, I climbed into my bed and thought about it again. I said the word and it's meaning over and over in my mind very slowly:

Infinity . . . Infinity . . . Infinity . . . Infinity . . . No beginning and no end . . . Infinity . . . Forever and ever . . . Infinity.

Suddenly, I felt as though I was floating in space, dangling in the darkness. I felt calm and overcome with a feeling of love and bliss. I accelerated faster and faster toward something drawing me in. I flew at warp speed through space for what seemed like forever until I saw the most amazing and enormous rotating ball of light off in the distance, and getting closer.

Billions of tiny pixels of energy were all vibrating together to make one giant orb, and I slowed down as I was drawn into the energy. The light surrounded me, and I was overcome with clarity and knowledge that I was completely connected to the whole.

"*Wow*! I *am* one of the pulsating pixels of energy! I am love. I am energy and light. I am connected. I understand. I remember. I am."

Just as suddenly as I left, I was back in my room, lying in my bed covered with my yellow blanket.

I had experienced something incredible, but because I never heard people talk about things like this, I didn't share it with anyone. I kept it a secret out of fear that everyone would think I was crazy.

A lot of life has happened since that night in my bedroom. I grew up. I struggled with severe depression, experienced financial hardship, was a single parent to a sometimes-challenging teenager and endured a scary surgery.

For days and weeks and years, I sometimes completely forgot and abandoned my truth, but I reclaim it today by sharing it with others.

A health scare a few years ago reminded me that although I am infinite, my body is not. The amount of time we have in this form on Earth is finite. It shook me up enough that I decided to start living my life as an experiment.

If I am terrified of something or think I can't do it, I try it! I swore I couldn't run. I took up running and ran a 633-day streak. I was terrified of embarrassing myself. I took improv classes and joined a troupe. Now I embarrass myself regularly on stage. I had social anxiety. I joined a women's group and traveled to Toronto to meet complete strangers. I stayed in an Airbnb with three women I had never met. It was fabulous, and we planned another trip together!

Each new experience continues to remind me that the present moment is a gift.

I believe we are infinite beings, and we have been gifted this short life on Earth to experiment with and experience every moment. It helps me put it all in perspective.

I am reminded that, in the words of the Indigo Girls, "It's only life after all."

*"These small yet simple shifts
mean big changes in my life."*

Grace, Growth and Giggles
Sol Farias

On a snowy night, when I was 8 years old, I was awoken by a knock at our front door at 3:00 am. I was at the top of the stairs watching my mom's profile as she opened the door to a police officer. My cheeks felt a sting of cold air that bustled through. After a few moments, my mom closed the door and collapsed to her knees. She belted out cries I had never heard before. It was at that moment that my life completely changed.

My dad was in a car accident. He was gone.

My mom took on two jobs in order to support our family. I would come home to an empty house and be alone until the babysitter dropped off my younger brother, Salvador. There were many rules I had to follow to keep us safe.

Don't answer the phone if it rings.
Don't answer the door if anyone knocks.
Don't turn on the stove.

Only eat cereal or sandwiches.
Keep certain lights on and others off, and rotate them.

Going to bed was the worst part because I was scared of the dark, but at least we slept together in my mom's big bed.

Fast forward 25 years and I was married to my true love, I had three beautiful children and I was grateful for it all.

Except, I felt like I didn't have any fun in my life. I couldn't enjoy it. I felt alone while making sure the kids were taken care of, the house was clean, the bills were paid and the property was maintained. My marriage started to sour, and I was constantly frustrated and angry.

Years continued to pass. Each day, when I came home from work, my kids would scream, "Mami's home!" and run to hug me. But as I hugged them into my chest, I'd gaze over their shoulders and fixate on the piles of shoes and coats on the floor, the piles of dirty dishes in the sink and the crumbs that were visible on the couch.

"Why are there shoes scattered from the doorway to the kitchen?"
"Why aren't the coats and backpacks hanging on the hooks?"
"Are the hooks broken?"
"Am I a broken record?"
"Why isn't anyone helping me?"

After losing my dad at 8, I wanted some sort of order in my life, but every day, I felt like I was failing. Nothing was getting better. One day, my son Mateo came home from school; he was upset about a spat with a good friend. I asked him to share with me, but he wouldn't.

"Why won't you just tell me what happened?!?" I asked him, frustrated that he wouldn't tell me. He said, "Mom, why do you always yell?

I made a mistake; I'd talk to you about it, but you are impossible!"

I just stopped. My heart dropped, and my world seemed to crumble all around me.

I knew he was right.

Why would anyone share with me when I was like a raging bull ready to charge? With crystal clear clarity, I saw who I had become, and I despised her. Overwhelming sadness washed over me. I knew things had to change.

Enough is enough.

I did the only thing I knew to do, and I called my lifelong friend, Christine. I broke my silence and shared it all.

"How did I get here?"
"I am so impossible to deal with."
"I don't want to live like this anymore."

With much love in her heart, she said over and over again, "Give yourself some grace, Sol."

Christine then introduced me to her great friend and transformational coach, Maya. Maya and her beautiful community support me as I learn to have grace with myself.

I learn to own and celebrate my mistakes as I grow.
I learn to feel my feelings.
I learn not to shame and blame and judge myself anymore.
I learn to be a little bit better every day.
I learn to laugh and play and be silly more often.

These small yet simple shifts mean big changes in my life. I can *finally* see the mom and the human being I want to be. I can have the thing I most desire—healthy, loving and thriving relationships with my children. Relationships where my children share with me the exciting and challenging parts of their school day; where we talk and communicate our feelings; where we laugh at our own silliness; and where we share our big dreams while feeling supported by one another.

Just recently, while I was at work, I called my son Mateo who told me that he was working on his homework project. I discovered, however, that he was not being honest with me. He was gaming instead. I was upset about his dishonesty. So, I texted him two Memojis: an angry Memoji and an angry face with white smoke fuming from the nostrils. "The smoke coming from my nostrils is *not* white light," I told him.

I had been teaching my children to inhale God's white light and exhale all that doesn't serve them at any moment they felt they needed to calm their body. I had also been teaching them to imagine opening up their crown chakra (the top of their head) and picture God's white light coming through them to love and support them.

I recognized that my instinct was to get angry and yell. So, I texted him again—with two different Memojis showing that I was trying to remain calm.

He replied with his own mind-blowing Memoji and stated, "Sending you all the white light from the crown of my head." I was so tickled and giggled the rest of my workday.

When I got home, he said, "I'm sorry mom" and gave me a big hug. It was so touching. He understood how I felt, and I could understand him too. I didn't have to hide my feelings of disappointment, and we could have giggles in the process. It doesn't mean I will never get angry, but we are now more open to communicate further.

I believe that through a little bit of grace we can grow and shift in every experience to give space for tender moments and giggles.

"'I love you,' I said to myself as I looked in the mirror."

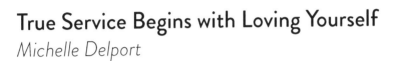

True Service Begins with Loving Yourself
Michelle Delport

When I was a little girl growing up in South Africa, I was a ball of energy—bouncing off walls, doing cartwheels and handstands and climbing trees. I could hardly sit still. I was the second youngest of six children: Michael, Clare, Victor, Emmy, myself and Anton. I was tasked with looking out for my sister Emmy who, although 18 months older than me, had a hearing impairment. But I loved to help.

One day, when I was bouncing about, my dad yelled at me to stop. "You are such a nincompoop," he said. "You are so stupid, aren't you, Michelle!?"

"Yes, Daddy, I am stupid. I am a nincompoop," I replied.

"That's right," he would say. He taught me well.

I learned to curb my excitement around him so he wouldn't get upset with me. I hated that he taught me to call myself names. I wanted his approval and would do anything to get it. I fetched his drinks and snacks. I handed him his tools while he worked. Soon, I was no longer a bouncing ball of energy.

Then, when I was 10 years old, he walked out. My father walked out on me. He walked out on my mom. He walked out on us all. In order to care for us, my mom had to pick up additional work, so I needed to help out even more. Michael and Clare were dyslexic; Victor was born with a narrow esophagus, so he was a walking choking hazard; Emmy was hard of hearing and needed extra love and patience so she didn't feel excluded; and Anton was only 3, so he needed a lot of attention. I was pretty much "normal," so I was expected to help with everyone else whenever I could.

For the next 16 years, I did what I have always done—made people comfortable and made sure that everyone's needs were met but my own. I even bought a pub at the age of 26 in the center of Amsterdam. I did what I knew how to do. I served everyone but myself.

I made customers comfortable.
I gave tourists tips and poured drinks.
I was a gifted hostess.
I anticipated people's every need and loved making them happy.

Every day, I got ready to smile, to entertain, to support and to serve.

One day, my friend Nancy called me. Her relationship had ended, and she was left to fend for herself with young twin girls. I told her, "Nancy, you are strong. You already provide for yourself and your older son. You are resilient and an outstanding, loving mother." I encouraged her to see how powerful she truly was.

More friends came to me for support during their challenging times. Each time I taught someone to be kinder to themselves, I was ignited. I started to glimpse the old Michelle—energetic, happy to be alive, happy to serve. The more people I supported, the more I came alive.

"This is it!" I realized.

I threw myself into personal development. I took all sorts of courses, read books, did workshops—anything to understand my purpose and my passion. The more I learned about myself, the happier I became. I peeled back layer upon layer of myself. I became more of the woman that I was put here to be.

I was introduced to mirror work when I recognized I needed to love myself more. The first time I looked at myself in the mirror, I just saw the old labels: "stupid" and "nincompoop." I sobbed for what felt like hours. Finally, as I looked into the mirror, the labels fell away, and I saw the truth of the woman before me. The woman that served her family. The woman that loved each of her siblings with all her heart. The woman that tried so hard for so long to gain everyone else's approval. And as I looked in the mirror, falling in love with the woman before me for the very first time, I finally realized the only approval I ever needed was my own.

"I love you," I said to myself as I looked in the mirror.

Over the next couple of years, as I kept doing the work, I shed layers of not being enough. I did more of the things that I loved. I started to skip and bounce around for no reason again. People came to me for support because they wanted to experience a similar change. And I loved helping them! I loved to serve from a place of love.

Soon after, I sold my bar, and I became a coach. I now have the honor and privilege of supporting others so that they can live a life they love and serve others without sacrificing themselves.

I believe that in order to truly be of service to others, we must first love ourselves.

"I realized that the moment I started loving myself,
I began living again!"

The Secret to Living Is Loving
Ramone Butler

When I was a little girl, I had the most vivid imagination. I would dream *big* dreams. I believed that I could do *anything* or be *anyone* I wanted. I was always giggling, laughing and joyful. I was going to help change the world. First, I wanted to be an attorney because I thought they could change the world. Then it was a forensic detective because I loved to solve mysteries. I always knew I was different, and that I was destined for great things; I just didn't know what. Over the years, though, people didn't understand my dreams, and they would tell me, "Get your head out of the clouds" or "You need to be realistic."

Forty years passed, and the dreams completely faded. My imagination disappeared and my health deteriorated. I was alone, depressed, angry and judgmental. I pushed away everyone I was close to. I hadn't done anything I'd dreamt of. I wasn't an attorney or a forensic detective. I wasn't even close. My body was a bag of bones, and I had a mass growing inside my belly. My life felt like a pile of *shit*!

I laid quietly in my dirty unmade bed with tears streaming down my face. I pleaded and prayed to God, something I had not done in decades.

Is this all there is, and then I die?
What am I here for?
What is my purpose?
What happened to all those big dreams?
Where is that happy and joyful little girl with the vivid imagination?
Please, please, please, God, help me turn my life around.

Days later, I finally accepted my sister's invitation to help me clean my home. I had been too embarrassed to accept before, but I knew things needed to change. It took us three full days. That was the beginning of my 540-degree turnaround.

Over the next year, we had an intervention. I changed everything. I started really taking care of myself, my health and my life. I made an appointment to see the doctor about the mass growing in my belly. I was diagnosed with Graves' disease, and the mass was a cancerous ovarian cyst that was 13 pounds when it was removed.

I started to get healthy again.
I sold my house.
I bought a new beautiful home.
I started walking.
I wrote in a gratitude journal everyday.
I did the things I loved every day.
I bought new clothes.
I bought new jewelry.
I started to laugh again!

With every new decision to love myself, invest in myself and do the things I loved, my life changed.

I realized that the moment I started *loving* myself, I began *living* again!

One day, while I was doing my personal development work on the computer, Tony Robbins came across my screen. I heard him speak, and I was so inspired that I ran into the lounge room and said to my Mum, "I finally found someone who speaks with passion like me!!!"

I realized that I was not crazy, I was not nuts. It's true that you can feel this way, you can love this way and you can dream this way!

Soon after, on a Zoom call, I spotted Maya Comerota, and she inspired me so much that I said to myself, "One day I will work with her." Now, I am honored to say that I do and that I am part of a group of courageous women around the world that live lives of love and service.

I have learned much and have fallen in love with the woman I am in the mirror. I have started to dream again. Not only that, but I dream *big* dreams, and I support other women doing the same.

I believe the secret to living is loving. And once you fall in love with yourself, you will fall in love with life.

"I was going to do everything
I could to live a life I truly loved."

Choose to Live a Life You Love
Shelly Oberg

It was 2002. I was a young mom to two beautiful children, Scott and Debra. I was doing everything I thought I was supposed to do.

I sang in the choir.
I taught Sunday school.
I volunteered for the library, the town and the school.
I had homemade meals on the table.
I kept a perfect house.
I tried to be the perfect wife.

I was trying to be it all and do it all, and I was struggling. I was struggling with a job and a marriage that was in turmoil. I was doing *everything*, and yet I was not happy. I did what everyone told me I should do—all the stuff—trying to keep it all afloat. I didn't even realize that I was dying inside.

On June 30, 2002, the phone rang. I answered. It was my best friend, JoAnn. "Shelly," she said, "Chris's plane is missing." Chris, her husband

and a good friend, had been out in New Mexico dropping water on the wildfires. I pulled on my clothes and ran over to their house.

Moments later, I was on the floor holding his little girl, Laura, on my lap. We were rocking together while I prayed, "Please God, please God, let Chris be okay. Please God, let Chris be okay."

The phone rang again—the voice on the other end said that the plane went down in a storm. JoAnn, Laura and I knelt, holding hands in prayer, crying together until Chris's brother Tim walked in the door with the news:

There were no survivors.

That sunny day in June I saw just how precious and short life is. I realized our lives could end at any moment, and I was in shock. Life could be over just like that. I asked myself, "Am I truly *living*?" I knew the answer.

No. I am not.

Chris was just 45! I was 40. I contemplated my life, and I realized that *I hadn't even lived yet*. So, then and there, I made a decision to change. I decided that I was going to do everything I could to live a life I truly loved.

A few months later, I threw some clothes in a black trash bag and walked out.

I walked out on being perfect.
I walked out on doing it all.
I walked out on trying to make everyone else happy.
I walked out on living life for everyone but myself.

I left to figure out how to create a life I really loved. I didn't know what to do or how I was going to do it, but I knew that what I had been doing wasn't working, and no way, no how would it end like that.

Did I make mistakes? Absolutely. Did I disappoint people? Yes. I made decisions that not everybody understood, and that was ok. It wasn't easy for anyone. But today I can say that I am actually *living*. So it was worth it.

Today, I live in Santo Tomas, Mexico, with my husband and best friend, Doug. We recently drove the Samurai to the beach with two of our granddaughters to search for sand dollars. The sun sparkled on the waves, and laughter filled the air with our silliness. As I walked in the surf with those two beautiful girls, my heart was full, and I knew *this* was the feeling of freedom. *This* was the peaceful "knowing" that I am living fully present and fully alive.

I now know that if you choose every single day to live a life you love—and you act on it—that anything is possible.

"That little voice of longing stuck with me, nudging me."

Blue Horizon
Marg Yungwirth

As a little girl, I grew up on a dairy farm in Honeymoon, Saskatchewan, with my 10 brothers and sisters: Ralph, Christopher, Teresa, Kasper, Alex, Joe, Eddie, Patrick and Patricia (the twins), myself and Stephen. I dreamed of being a famous singer and performing on the big stage like Dolly Parton, Martina McBride and the Dixie Chicks.

When I wasn't milking cows, feeding calves, cleaning the barns or cooking the meals for our big hungry family, I was either singing or playing with my brothers and sisters—swinging from the rafters in the hay loft.

Life on the farm was never boring!

We even had a family band called the Hordyski Family. Eddie was the lead singer, and Patty and I sang harmony. We performed in local talent shows and on TV shows.

Once my older brothers left home, my workload piled up. There was less and less time to play and sing. I had calves to feed, a barn to clean. I had hay to bale and milk tanks to sanitize. I think I was the only kid who actually loved going to school because that was *my* time. I could see my friends, play and not have to take care of the farm.

After graduating, I met the love of my life, Leonard, a farmer. By the age of 21, we were married, even though I swore I would never marry a farmer! I'd had enough of the farm, or so I thought! We quickly started a family and had three beautiful children: Kanden, Shaelene and Lindee.

For the next 30 years, the workload on our farm grew. I worked part-time *and* managed the family, the house and the farm. Each day, there was seeding, harvesting, running around with the kids, gardening and yard work.

It seemed that there was no more time for fun or singing. That little girl who used to swing from the rafters and had big dreams of being a famous singer was a distant memory.

I yearned for *more*. But a part of me felt guilty. I already had so much. Yet, something was missing. What was I longing for? That little voice of longing stuck with me, nudging me.

One day my daughter Shaelene brought my granddaughter Bentlee over. I took her into the orchard where she ran ahead of me, calling, "Come on Baba run, you can do it, we're a team!"

We played music and danced. She would giggle, and I would too. I felt a spark in me. The spark of *more*. The spark of fun! I remembered the me that used to play, laugh and giggle.

I wanted more of *that*!

Each time the grandkids—Adelyn, Lydia, Emmett, Bentlee, Lincoln, Hazel and Holden—came over, we would crank up the tunes and listen to songs from my cds like "Landslide" by the Dixie Chicks or "Blue Horizon" by Farmer's Daughter. I had sung "Blue Horizon" when I was in a band years before. When I played the song for the grandkids, I sang for the first time in many years.

But if I could sail away, leave this all behind
Find peace inside my mind
I would ride the wind, lose all touch with time
I wouldn't say goodbye
I'd go until the ocean meets the sky
Blue horizon

They all looked at me, in awe, with their big, beautiful eyes and said, "Baba, you have such a beautiful voice." My heart swelled, and a part of me ignited. I remembered how I loved to dance and sing on stage.

Around that same time, my coach and beautiful friend, Maya Comerota, asked me a couple simple yet powerful questions:

"What would you love?" she asked. "What would bring you joy?"

And just like that, I remembered.

I loved to sing!
I loved to dance!
I loved to play!
I loved to laugh!
Yes!!!
That was it!!!

The *more* I was looking for was having more fun and doing the things that I loved to do!

So, that very day, I made a promise to myself:

Marg, it is time to have some fun! No more being so busy that you forget to do what lights you up!

I believe that when we stop doing so much and start playing a lot more, we really live!

So, if you see a girl rockin' out in her car, singing "Blue Horizon" and dancing in the street, that's probably me.

ABOUT THE CURATOR

*"Maya is a reigning example that we all have a story.
It's just knowing how to package it and offer it.
Maya is the example of how to make it real.
If you are searching to be the person you were born to be,
she's your girl."*

— *Dean Graziosi*

Maya Comerota is a luminary, visionary entrepreneur and top transformational teacher and coach on a mission to unlock human potential.

She has built multibillion dollar initiatives and seven-figure companies. She has supported over 1.5 million people worldwide to live a life they love living and make seemingly impossible dreams a reality.

Maya is an expert at personal innovation with certifications from the world's leaders in high performance, neuroscience and life mastery.

As a highly sought after speaker, Maya has been invited to speak on stages with Tony Robbins, Mary Morrissey, Dean Graziosi, Bo Eason and Kyle Cease, among others. She has also been a featured expert on television networks such as NBC, ABC and CBS, and featured in publications such as *Entrepreneur Magazine* and *Entrepreneur Mindset*.

She was recently a featured speaker on Richard Branson's island and Tony Robbins' and Dean Graziosi's Project Next.

Maya is the CEO of 528HzInc and the creator of Born For This Elite Coaching, Living Legendary Mastermind and The Living Luminary Mastermind.

As a high performance consultant and coach, Maya has worked with NFL athletes, entrepreneurs, executives and fortune 100 companies such as AbbVie, Abbott, Shire, Baxter, Quintiles (now IQVIA) and the Magic Johnson Foundation.

Her greatest accomplishment, however, is being a devoted wife to her husband, James, and a proud Mom to her son, Hunter.

To connect with Maya, visit mayacomerota.com.

Do you have a story that you long to share? A message to share with the world?

Would you like to participate in the next
When Love Speaks compilation?

Visit mayacomerota.com to learn more about becoming a Featured Author in the next *When Love Speaks* collection.

It is time to live and leave your legacy.